INTERPRETING
THE
TIMES

INTERPRETING
THE
TIMES

CHUCK D. PIERCE

Charisma
HOUSE
A STRANG COMPANY

INTERPRETING THE TIMES by Chuck D. Pierce
Published by Charisma House
A Strang Company
600 Rinehart Road
Lake Mary, Florida 32746
www.strangbookgroup.com

Design Director: Bill Johnson
Cover design by Marvin Eans

This publication is translated in Spanish under the title *Cómo interpretar los
tiempos,* copyright © 2008 by Chuck D Pierce, published by Casa Creación, a
Strang company. All rights reserved.

Library of Congress Cataloging-in-Publication Data

Pierce, Chuck D., 1953-
Interpreting the times / Chuck Pierce. -- 1st ed.
p. cm.
Includes bibliographical references.
ISBN 978-1-59979-198-2
1. Time--Religious aspects--Christianity. I. Title.
BT78.P54 2008
236--dc22

2007032373

First Edition

09 10 11 12 13—9 8 7 6 5 4 3 2
Printed in the United States of America

CONTENTS

CHAPTER 1

DEVELOPING AN UNDERSTANDING OF TIME

HAVE YOU EVER NOTICED HOW OFTEN WE USE THE WORD *TIME* in our everyday conversation? Not only are we acutely aware of the passage of time, but also our speech is littered with references to the characteristics of time and our lack of it. We refer to time in countless expressions and figures of speech, so we are obviously preoccupied with the concept.

Consider some of the ways we reference time:

- "Time waits for no man."
- "Time is money."
- "Time marches on."
- "You're wasting time."
- "Time is of the essence."
- "In the nick of time."
- "I am pressured because of lack of time."
- "I do not have enough hours in a day."

Celestial bodies—the sun, moon, planets, and stars—have provided us a reference for measuring the passage of time throughout the existence of mankind. Ancient civilizations relied upon the apparent motion of these bodies through the sky to determine seasons, months, and years. We know little about the details of timekeeping in prehistoric eras, but wherever we turn up records and artifacts, we usually discover that in every culture there was someone preoccupied with measuring and recording the passage of time. There was such a fascination with light, day, dark, and night that whole worship systems were formed around time!

Ice Age hunters in Europe more than twenty thousand years ago scratched lines and gouged holes in sticks and bones, possibly counting the days between phases of the moon. Five thousand years ago, Sumerians in the Tigris-Euphrates valley in modern-day Iraq had a calendar that divided the year into thirty-day months, divided the day into twelve periods (each corresponding to two of our hours), and divided these periods into thirty parts (each like four of our minutes). We have no written records of Stonehenge, built more than four thousand years ago in England, but its alignments show that its purposes apparently included the determination of seasonal or celestial events, such as lunar eclipses, solstices, and so on.[1]

Most people hold one of two views on the meaning of time. The *realist's view*, which was espoused by Sir Isaac Newton, maintains that time is linear and part of the fundamental structure of the universe. According to this view, time is a dimension that can be measured and contains a sequence of events. The contrasting view of time, embraced by Gottfried Leibniz and Immanuel Kant, contends that time is part of a mental measuring system and cannot be objectively measured. According to this concept, time is not a line along which objects and events move sequentially, but rather it is an intellectual way to measure events. In other words, time isn't a "real," measurable thing.

Beyond these two views of time and its measurement, there are other aspects of time that have intrigued man since the Garden of Eden. I love the first four chapters of Genesis. They are mysterious yet concrete. They develop the concept of family in space and time. One concept of time in the garden is the *cyclical* nature of time: *the repetition of seasons in nature and, consequently, in the life of man.*

There is the philosophical concept of time called *fatalism*. A good deal of work in the philosophy of time has been produced by people worried about fatalism, which can be understood as the thesis that *whatever will happen in the future is already unavoidable.* In other words, no human is able to prevent it from occurring. Oh, my! Wouldn't you hate to live with that philosophy of life? However, that could explain some people's negative attitudes. Many religious groups have adopted this belief of time. Why pray? Whatever is going to happen will happen, so just wait it out and hope for the best. Love God, but never trust Him to change the events of mankind. Just go blindly into the night, and perhaps day will break again.

There is the idea that time itself can be bridged. This idea includes the concept of time travel and marries time with space. In the children's classic by Madeleine L'Engle, *A Wrinkle in Time*, the protagonists in the story are transported through time and space by three angelic personages in order to rescue their father from an evil entity on another planet. In order to reach their extraterrestrial destination, these personages "wrinkle" time and space to shorten the time and distance between Earth and the planet of interest. In the chapter titled "The Tesseract," the "angels" explain how time and space are linear and can be folded back upon themselves, thereby shortening the distance between two points. This is interesting, but I am really not sure of the folding-back part of the theory. Fold back too much, and you will live in a world where you are not sure whether you are coming or going. Actually, déjà vu will become a confusing phenomenon.

Then, of course, there is the *Philip situation* in the Book of Acts! I love this. I do not fully understand the scenario in my mind, but I embrace the miraculous happening and know that God could do this again today. Philip was "caught away." Time and space were defied. The full account is given in Acts 8:38–40:

> So he commanded the chariot to stand still. And both Philip and the eunuch went down into the water, and he baptized him. Now when they came up out of the water, the Spirit of the Lord caught Philip away, so that the eunuch saw him no more; and he went on his way rejoicing. But Philip was found at Azotus. And passing through, he preached in all the cities till he came to Caesarea.

Philip completes one mission, prompted by the Spirit of God, and then is *caught up* and carried to another mission thirty-four miles away, ready to begin his next assignment. How could this happen? Did an angel carry him like in the science-fiction realm? As much as I travel, approximately two hundred thousand miles a year, I wish I could tap into this.

Questions to Ponder

Since so many are preoccupied with the concept of time, consider each of these questions:

- What is the right context of time?
- How can I interpret time if I do not even understand time?
- What if there was a time freeze?
- Is there such a phenomenon as time travel?
- Is time travel permitted by the laws of logic, nature, and metaphysics?
- Is our thinking about time and space too concrete?
- If the big bang theory was the true account of the beginning of the universe, did time begin with a big bang?
- Are space and time important?
- Can I move from one dimension of time into eternal time?

These questions can lead us into a realm of reasoning and actually get us in a loop that we cannot figure out. Therefore, let's get a little more personal.

- Does time control you?
- Can you *see* into a different dimension?

- Do you understand how to maneuver through societal change and not allow those changes to overtake you?

- Do you feel manipulated by time?

- Does time seem to be an enemy to you?

- Do you feel captured by time?

- Did some force change time around you and cause you to feel imprisoned by the change?

- Do you believe you have a future that is good?

- Does your present control your future?

- Does your past control your present and leave you confused about your future?

I could go on and on—and I will as we move through the pages ahead! Here is the real question that I want to address in the pages ahead: *Is there a Creator who transcends and enters time to commune with His children so they may efficiently walk in time?* When you mess up in one season, can He make you capable of redeeming the times or buying back wasted time? Can He extend your horizon line and give you a glimpse of what will be in days ahead? In the midst of evil days, can He reveal remedies that will cause man, His most marvelous creation, to walk without fear in victory?

I will choose this latter premise because the theory has become a reality in my own life. I will attempt to explain some of His ways that He has revealed to me in my short life journey with this wonderful Creator of time and space. In this book, I hope to help you make your transitions from one point in time to another, understanding that, by faith, you can succeed in crossing over into a new dimension of success.

I am known for being prophetic. Actually, the Bible says that we all prophesy. However, it is one thing to have a *sense* of what will happen in days ahead or to give wisdom and counsel for a present situation in life, but to *foretell* what is going to happen and have some recognition

Is there a Creator who transcends and enters time to commune with His children so they may efficiently walk in time?

of the time frame of the event is a remarkable miracle that could only come from a supernatural source. First Chronicles 12:32 says, "The children of Issachar who had understanding of the times, to know what Israel ought to do…" This will be the theme of this book. May this book help you to understand "time" and, more importantly, know what vital life-giving decisions need to be made from that understanding. As you read this book, may time move from being a philosophy or a curse to becoming a real gift from God. May you enter into a new reality of space, time, Spirit, and truth as you advance through the pages ahead.

I WILL RESTORE WHAT YOU HAVE LOST!

When I was a child, we lived about a mile from the main highway. I loved when my dad would come home from work. That meant that our family could go over to the land we owned, which was about ten miles away, to check on the cattle and horses and count the newborn calves. Each day after I got home from school and finished my homework, I would watch and wait with expectancy. I actually would sit underneath a large tree in our yard and listen carefully to the cars on the main highway. I could not see them, but I could hear them. I learned the sound of Dad's truck as it would slow on the highway almost three quarters of a mile away. If I could not hear his truck, I would grow anxious, not understanding why he was late and not *on time*. Our day would then have to be rearranged.

As time passed, he became less and less consistent in being *on time*. I continued to watch with anticipation for him to get home. Therefore, I became more and more anxious and disappointed when this did not happen as I hoped. I remember looking up into the sky one day and asking the Lord why my dad was not home, what had happened to him, was something wrong, and what had we done at home to make him go elsewhere and forsake our family.

Time became a reality, and the reality was linked with disappointment. Eventually our family life grew very difficult because my dad was now *out of time*. Instead of his being dependable and on time, he had lost the concept of time and responsibility. As a result, all we owned, as well as the relationship and trust that we had in him, disappeared. When he did arrive, the time was not joyous but filled with fighting, accusations, mistrust, and confusion. Life had taken a very peculiar, hurtful turn. I eventually stopped watching, and I lost the joy and expectancy of his coming.

My dad, who had all the potential to succeed in everything he touched, a man who was favored by many and who had gained the inheritance of his family's family, was now captured by the enemy of corruption. Out of time and boundaries, he eventually died a very destructive, premature death at the age of thirty-nine. I somehow knew that it was not God's plan for his life to have been shortened and his inheritance to be left in shambles.

But God! He can break through darkness and intervene with His voice to re-create circumstances and redeem time. His voice entered into my life in a hospital room. As if reverberating through a mountainous cavern, His words rang inside me: "I can restore what you have lost." They echoed throughout my entire being, becoming my lifeline. His words even began a process in my re-creation. Almost instantly I could sense a breaking of the power of loss that was being held within my genetic structure. This was the very power creating infirmity and disease within my body. He had come into time in the hospital room where I was under oxygen, and in that NOW moment had taken up my cause.

As I explained earlier, because our family had experienced one trauma after another, I was wounded like a hurt animal afraid of embracing or being embraced. In a condition like this, one does not really know how to change. So many times we become self-destructive. Our soul is fragmented, our spirit is broken, and our body reflects the pain of the situation. Now, here I was hospitalized and diagnosed with double pneumonia and an enlarged heart.

I love people who pray and speak the Word. My mother's mother, Inez LaGrone, a very godly but tough pioneer type of a woman, had warned me that the Lord had never intended me to stray and go the direction that my dad had gone. I was young, in college, knew more than everyone, and was rapidly straying toward the things I hated the most. These were the same patterns that had been used by the enemy to destroy my dad. She said these words: "I refuse for you to not accomplish your destiny, so I will just ask the Lord to deal with you." The next thing I knew, I was collapsed and in the hospital. Of course, my grandmother was one of the nurses at the hospital. She came in my room and said, "I told you this would happen."

BUT GOD! By His sovereign hand, He placed me in a room with a Pentecostal pastor! This man introduced me to a person I did not know: the Holy Spirit! I had accepted Christ years before, and yet through this pastor, the person of Christ suddenly became alive to me. Not only did the Lord seem so real and near to me, so did His Word. I began to devour Scripture like never before.

In that meeting at the hospital, the Lord showed me the war that was going on inside me. There was a war with my evil nature. There was a war with sin domination. There was a war concerning my family and all its downfalls and failings. There was a war with my inheritance. There was even a war with my faith! But the voice of the Lord had shaken my circumstances and now my times had changed.

You Will Understand Time

We wander through life and really don't understand what we are doing each day. I believe that many of us get up and go through the motions some days and never really expect God to do anything.

Two passages of Scripture are very important life forces in my daily walk with the Lord. Matthew 7:7–12 says:

Ask, and it will be given to you; seek, and you will find; knock, and it will be opened to you. For everyone who asks receives, and he who seeks finds, and to him who knocks it will be opened. Or what man is there among you who, if his son asks for bread, will give him a stone? Or if he asks for a fish, will he give him a serpent? If you then, being evil, know how to give good gifts to your children, how much more will your Father who is in heaven give good things to those who ask Him! Therefore, whatever you want men to do to you, do also to them, for this is the Law and the Prophets.

After reading the testimony that I just wrote, you can probably see that God had to restore in me an expectation to ask, watch, and wait until He answered. He had to redo my entire concept of Father's love. Even though the relationship with my earthly father decayed, I can't say that he did not love me. His affections and desires had just been so misdirected that he lost the ability to express the power of love to the family with whom God had blessed him. However, after God visited me, He showed me His love. He also revealed to me the love that He had for my earthly father.

God brought the emotion that He had for my father—which had been rejected in one time frame—and allowed me to experience the power of that emotion in another time frame.

This came in a very peculiar way. I was driving to work in downtown Houston, and the presence of God filled the car. I said, "Lord, this love is overwhelming! What have I done to deserve this?"

The Spirit of God then spoke to me, saying, "This is the love I had for your father. Even though he never experienced the fullness of what I intended to pour out upon him, you can experience that NOW in your life!" Somehow God brought the emotion that He had for my father—which had been rejected in one time frame—and allowed me to experience the power of that emotion in another time frame. This changed my whole view of all the pain that I had experienced from the terrible situations that had occurred in my family. Because God had met me in this NOW time, I was able to look back at another time and place and see His true view of the situation. This was very, very healing.

This experience created a new faith in me to pray. The verses from Matthew 7 became reality to me. Through the years I have matured in asking, seeking, knocking, and expecting the Lord, in His time, to come and bring a manifestation of what I am hoping for.

The second important life force scripture is Jeremiah 33:3. I like what the Amplified Bible says:

> Call to Me and I will answer you and show you great and mighty things, fenced in and hidden, which you do not know (do not distinguish and recognize, have knowledge of and understand).

I believe that we must learn to cry out to the Lord. God, who is not in time, comes down into our time and begins to act. I love this verse! When He enters our time, He begins to reveal things to us that we could never recognize or have knowledge of without His intervention. By His Spirit we are connected to the Father of time. Therefore, He can reveal anything necessary for us to *see* in our generational cycle of time.

I went to a meeting in the late 1970s. At that time, there was not much talk about the prophetic in my circles. At this meeting a well-known prophet spoke. In his message he said the following, directing the words toward me: "You will understand time, and you will help My people walk in My perfect timing." Something quickened deep within my heart. Right then, I didn't understand the concept of time at all, although by this time in my life I was very aware of God's presence and intervention. However, He was about to take me on a journey that would teach me about time and about walking in His timing. Not only would He use this in my life, but He would also use me in days ahead to help many others understand times and seasons.

GOD AND TIME

God is not subject to the limitations imposed on us by linear time. C. S. Lewis, in *Mere Christianity*, wrote the following explanation concerning God and time:

> Almost certainly God is not in Time. His life does not consist of moments following one another. If a million people are praying to Him at ten-thirty tonight, He need not listen to them all in that one little snippet which we call ten-thirty. Ten-thirty—and every other moment from the beginning of the world—is always the Present for him. If you like to put it that way, He has all eternity in which to listen to the split second of prayer put up by a pilot as his plane crashes in flames....All the days are "Now" for Him. He does not remember you doing things yesterday; He simply sees you doing them, because, though you have lost yesterday, He has not.[2]

By considering this characteristic of God, you will realize that your heavenly Father has access to every moment in your life from beginning to end as though they were the present. By the Holy Spirit, you can actually access those times in your past when you felt abandoned, abused, betrayed, fearful, happy, fulfilled, or any other emotion or condition. Not only can you be forgiven for the past, but you can also travel back in time with God, see Him as a "very present help" (Ps. 46:1) in the past, and redeem those times from the past that the enemy wanted to use for evil.

My wife's favorite Scripture passage is Ephesians 5:8–16:

> For you were once darkness, but now you are light in the Lord. Walk as children of light (for the fruit of the Spirit is in all goodness, righteousness, and truth), finding out what is acceptable to the Lord. And have no fellowship with the unfruitful works of darkness, but rather expose them. For it is shameful even to speak of those things which are done by them in secret. But all things that are exposed are made manifest by the light, for whatever makes manifest is light. Therefore He says: "Awake, you who sleep, arise

from the dead, and Christ will give you light." See then that you walk circumspectly, not as fools but as wise, *redeeming the time,* because the days are evil.

—EMPHASIS ADDED

To *redeem* means to buy back or to be released from prison. This scripture is so important to Pam because her past was very destructive. After living with alcoholic parents the first twelve years of her life, she was then adopted—a wonderful blessing. This began the "buying back" season of her life. You can read about many of her experiences in my book *One Thing.*[3]

We can't ignore our history where mistakes occur, but we can connect from the present back to the past and then realign our future.
—Dutch Sheets

This is one of the functions of the power of salvation and deliverance: *redeeming the past from the hand of the enemy so it is no longer a weapon against us.* The concept of how to restore your wasted years and buy back time will be addressed in my next book.

Dutch Sheets, a dear friend and Christian leader with whom I have spent many hours in ministry, says this about time: "Before we fell from grace in the garden, God had already decreed how He would fix our mistakes."[4]

Revelation 13:8 says, "All who dwell on the earth will worship him, whose names have not been written in the Book of Life of the Lamb slain from the foundation of the world." In other words, the Lord had already made provision for the mistake that man was to make. I don't think He wanted man to listen to the enemy and break communion with Him. However, I think He made a provision before the foundation of the world so that when we mess up in time, He can restore us back to His eternal plan. Dutch goes on to say in his teaching, "We can't ignore our history where mistakes occur, but we can connect from the present back to the past and then realign our future."[5] Later in this book I will explain why Dutch is so confident when he makes this statement.

FAITH IS ALWAYS NOW!

Sometimes we lose the reality of NOW! One of the best biblical examples of NOW is the story of the Syrophoenician women in Mark 7:24–30 (TLB):

> Then he left Galilee and went to the region of Tyre and Sidon, and tried to keep it a secret that he was there, but couldn't. For as usual the news of his arrival spread fast. Right away a woman came to him whose little girl was possessed by a demon. She had heard about Jesus and now she came and fell at his feet, and pled with him to release her child from the demon's control. (But she was Syrophoenician—a "despised Gentile!") Jesus told her, "First I should help my own family—the Jews. It isn't right to take the children's food and throw it to the dogs." She replied, "That's true, sir, but even the puppies under the table are given some scraps from the children's plates." "Good!" he said, "You have answered well—so well that I have healed your little girl. Go on home, for the demon has left her!" And when she arrived home, her little girl was lying quietly in bed, and the demon was gone.

This passage is so incredible. When you think of the context of what is happening, the faith element involved in the Syrophoenician woman's actions is quite breathtaking. Jesus is visiting Tyre and Sidon, and while He is there, this non-Jewish woman begins to beg Him to touch her daughter. Jesus explains to her that He did not come to Tyre or Sidon or the world at that point in time to bless the Gentiles, but rather, His mission from Father was to touch the Jews and cause this people to recognize that Messiah was in their midst. Then He equated the Gentiles and this woman with "a dog" (unclean).

The woman could have gotten so offended by this that she might have left the house and prevented Father from intervening in the earth realm. Instead, the woman says to Jesus that she understands His mission, but that even dogs can eat crumbs if they fall from the table of the feast.

In other words, she said: "I know this is not Your NOW time for us Gentiles, but I need a miracle NOW!"

Jesus could not do or say anything on Earth that Father did not show Him to do or say. So Father responded from heaven, came into time, and literally expanded the mission of Jesus at that moment. The Lord said, "You have answered well—so well that I have healed your little girl. Go on home, for the demon has left her!" Our faith can cause the situations in time to shift.

Time: A Ruling Force in Our Mind

Because of our humanity, time has more control over our lives than it should. It is essential that you take your place above the linear timeline and see from God's perspective. When you do that, you begin to understand that you are a citizen of an eternal kingdom visiting a temporal dimension. It is the cares of this world that tend to make the temporal seem more real than the eternal. I will explain this concept as we venture through the course of this book.

When we traveled on the Fifty-State Tour, Dutch would discuss time and realignment. His main message to the nation was: "God is snapping many things back in order that have been out of order." Then he would proceed to teach about time. His favorite scripture was Isaiah 46:10, which says, "Declaring the end from the beginning, and from ancient times things that are not yet done, saying, 'My counsel shall stand, and I will do all My pleasure.'" Another version of this verse says, "My purpose will be established, and I will accomplish all My good pleasure'" (NASU). He always tied this verse to Job 22:28: "You will also decree a thing, and it will be established for you; and light will shine on your ways" (NASU). In other words, he was teaching that you can decree a thing, and it will manifest and give light to your path. God can show you something in the past, and you can make that declaration into another time frame. Then in that season, light comes and explodes in your path.

In *Releasing the Prophetic Destiny of a Nation*, I share that:

A *decree* is an official order, edict, or decision. A decree is something that seems to be foreordained. This is what makes decrees prophetic. *Decree* can also mean to order, decide, or officially appoint a group or person to accomplish something. A decree is linked with setting apart or ordaining something or someone. A *declaration* is the act of announcing something or making a formal statement or proclamation. This statement sometimes is what a plaintiff releases in his complaint resulting in a court action. A *proclamation* actually brings something into a more official realm. A proclamation can ban, outlaw, or restrict. This is linked with the process of binding and loosing.

Once we hear the word of the Lord decreed, declared, or proclaimed, God begins to establish this word in the earth realm. This causes God's people to press in for a full manifestation of what He is longing to accomplish in our midst. All through the Word of God you find decrees, declarations, and proclamations. Cyrus sent out a decree that caused God's people to return from captivity and rebuild the city of Jerusalem and the temple of God. Caesar sent out a decree that positioned Mary and Joseph in the place where prophecy could be fulfilled through the birth of Jesus. Elijah declared that the heavens would be shut up. The priests proclaimed what God was ordaining.[6]

Each time you come into agreement with heaven and speak the will of Father into the earth, God's eternal time and plan re-sequences and realigns the earth.

STEPPING INTO TIME

Imagine for a moment that all of eternity is represented by a large piece of paper. This is where God is—unlimited by time and space. Now draw a line on that piece of paper that represents time with a beginning and an end. This line begins when God instituted time at Creation, and it will end when God says, "Time's up."

Man lives on the line, while God can step in and out of time according to His purposes and plans. God sees all of time at once and doesn't have to wait for anything to happen; all is *present* for Him. This is a simplified explanation of a complex idea, but it works. Because of God's position relative to time, He can—and often does—seem to answer our prayers before they have been uttered!

God has chosen us as the necessary link to bring His will from heaven to the earth. He wants us to commune with Him, listen carefully to His voice, gain prophetic revelation, and decree that revelation into the earth. This will unlock miracles and release His blessings. Once you hear God, you can intercede, but you can also prophesy. *Prophecy* is declaring His mind and His heart. As you speak, He forms His will in the earth. We should always be willing to say "yes and amen" to His promises. When you receive prophetic revelation, you need to decree the prophetic revelation, and then the atmosphere into which you decree goes on *heaven's time* instead of *Earth time.*

> *God sees all of time at once and doesn't have to wait for anything to happen; all is present for Him.*

OUR MISTAKES CAN SHIFT TIME!

Recently, Aaron Smith, my assistant, and I were flying from Syracuse to Chicago. I had been doing regional meetings across northern New York. Now it was time to fly to Chicago for the Feast of Tabernacles with a group of leaders in that city. When we initially flew from Dallas to Rochester, New York, we were on one type of regional jet. The bag that I purchased and used fit perfectly into the overhead bin of that jet. In Syracuse, I glanced out the window and thought, "We are on the same type of jet that we flew to New York on, so I will just carry my bag on with me since it fits so well in the overhead rather than check it at the gate." The gate agent asked me if I wanted to check my bag, and I said, "No, it fits perfectly." He gave me the strangest look.

Aaron even said, "Why don't you just check it?"

I said, "But it fits perfectly."

The gate agent came back a second time and asked, "Are you sure you don't want to take this ticket and check the bag before you get on the plane?"

I said, "It fits perfectly."

We got on the plane, and I just threw the bag up in the overhead. However, it got stuck. I then noticed this wasn't the exact type of plane we had flown on previously. This plane had only one seat on the right side instead of two. I tried to push the bag into the overhead, and it got stuck worse. At that point, the overhead began to collapse. Aaron then tried to help, but the overhead compartment dropped further down toward the seat in front of us. I could not get the bag in or out, and now the plane was broken. The flight attendant came back to help, and when he attempted to manipulate the bag, the overhead compartment completely fell. Oh, my! This was a nightmare, like one of those moments you see on *I Love Lucy*. The couple in front of me was laughing. A woman and child behind me were saying at that point they didn't care if we got to Chicago or not, but the man next to me was furious. We all had to deboard the plane while they spent over an hour attempting to fix the overhead. They finally used duct tape to get the overhead repositioned and back in place.

I was in horror. I had gotten a whole plane out of time. The flight connections of the other passengers were totally in chaos. It had been a long time since I repented and cried out to the Lord to forgive me for being so stubborn. I then asked Him to please reposition us back into His perfect timing. When we got to Chicago, we found out that most of the flights there had been delayed. Therefore, most of the passengers were back in time and on the way to their final destinations. This showed me the power of our mistakes and how they affect not only us but also many others around us.

Here is the Job passage that Dutch frequently spoke on:

> Quit quarreling with God! Agree with him and you will have peace
> at last! His favor will surround you if you will only admit that you
> were wrong. Listen to his instructions and store them in your heart.

If you return to God and put right all the wrong in your home, then you will be restored. If you give up your lust for money and throw your gold away, then the Almighty himself shall be your treasure; he will be your precious silver! Then you will delight yourself in the Lord and look up to God. You will pray to him, and he will hear you, and you will fulfill all your promises to him. Whatever you wish will happen! And the light of heaven will shine upon the road ahead of you. If you are attacked and knocked down, you will know that there is someone who will lift you up again. Yes, he will save the humble and help even sinners by your pure hands.

—Job 22:21–30, TLB

I really like it when it says, "Quit quarreling with God," and when it says that you can decree a decree and it will happen in the earth.

A PARALLEL UNIVERSE—
BACK TO THE FUTURE!

Most serious scientists dismiss the idea of *parallel universes* depicted in science fiction as "bad science" based on unobservable phenomena. Even so, there are those in the scientific community who entertain the possibility that science-fiction writers are not that far from the truth. In science fiction, the parallel universe device is often used as the basis for the story. In the 1990s, the television series *Sliders* revolved around the existence of parallel universes containing identical people and places in different stages of reality based on the choices or circumstances in each universe or dimension. The characters in the show "slid" from one reality to another and often encountered their "other selves" in different situations. Then, of course, there was the old series *The Twilight Zone*, which had you in and out of time zones in every show. I watched one episode when I was a kid and freaked out, so my mother was very cautious in not allowing me to watch this show much.

The concept of the parallel universe implies that there are other worlds running parallel to our own in which our doppelgangers (alter egos) live nearly identical lives to our own. In science fiction, the characters are able to access these other worlds through extraordinary devices, such as wormholes or "quantum portals." Now, with the Sci-Fi channel, there are so many shows to watch that sometimes we are not sure what world we are observing.

These are my wife's favorite type of shows. I cannot say I watch many, because by seeking God I have learned to enter spiritual portals that go beyond time and space. This is real to me. Therefore, fiction can become confusing at times when the power of the Holy Spirit is not involved in my communication with a holy God.

These kinds of literary devices posit that time travels in a linear fashion, but events along the line can be altered through different actions or choices. In *Back to the Future II*, the second movie in a three-movie series that now falls into the classic arena, Marty McFly, the main character, travels via the DeLorean time machine into the future for a specific purpose. Biff Tannen, Marty's archrival and enemy, "borrows" the DeLorean time machine to go back to the past in order to give his younger self a sports almanac from the future.

His younger self uses the statistical information in the almanac to amass a fortune through gambling, thus changing the events along the timeline. When Marty returns to the earlier time, everything has been changed because of Biff's success in gambling.

One decision can affect several generations. Bad decisions create genetic and environmental defects that must be restored to the Creator's original intent.

According to Doc Brown, Marty's genius, time-traveling companion, Biff created an alternate reality when he introduced the sports almanac into the past. This kind of alteration could be compared to diverting the flow of a river. When the river's course is changed—by a dam, for instance—the original river ceases to exist, and the new one creates an alternate riverbed. Now the only way for Marty to set things right and restore his own *river* to its course was to go back to the moment when young Biff acquired the almanac from his older self, get the book away from Biff, and make sure he never got the chance to use the information to make his fortune. When that happens, the original timeline is restored.

This is really a good example of how time works. Time is like a river; when dammed or its course is altered, the original path is changed, and the overall environment is affected. One decision can affect several generations. Bad decisions create genetic and environmental defects that must be restored to the Creator's original intent.

TIME AND SPACE: WHAT A BIG BANG!

Time is represented through change! Each night when we look at the moon, we think of time as the circular motion of the moon around the earth representing the changing of a day. The passing of time then enters into the concept of space. One of my favorite biblical passages is Acts 17:23–27, which says:

> Therefore, the One whom you worship without knowing, Him I proclaim to you: God, who made the world and everything in it, since He is Lord of heaven and earth, does not dwell in temples made with hands. Nor is He worshiped with men's hands, as though He needed anything, since He gives to all life, breath, and all things. And He has made from one blood every nation of men to dwell on all the face of the earth, and has determined their preappointed times and the boundaries of their dwellings, so that they should seek the Lord, in the hope that they might grope for Him and find Him, though He is not far from each one of us.

Very simply, this passage states that God knows our time and place; He "pro-horizoned" it. When you are at the right place at the right time, He extends your horizon so you can see much further into the future.

According to the theory of relativity, space, or the universe, emerged in the big bang some 13.7 billion years ago. Before that, all matter was packed into an extremely tiny dot. That dot also contained the matter that later came to be the sun, the earth, and the moon—the heavenly bodies that tell us about the passing of time. Before the big bang, there was no space or time.

A big bang! There has to be more to life than *kerplunk* and here we are! Kari Enqvist, professor of cosmology at the University of Helsinki, says, "In the theory of relativity, the concept of time begins with the Big Bang the same way as parallels of latitude begin at the North Pole. You cannot go further north than the North Pole."[7] But before the North Pole and before time, there was God!

The way we view time is somehow developed by how we are aligning and ordering the temporal happenings, events, and circumstances around us. We add all of these events up and make a whole perception of something and then define that as *time*. This has some credibility in our view of life, but it perhaps does not fully grasp the nature of God and His plan of fullness for us. This is using physics to define time instead of determining that time is the basis for physics.

Let me illustrate with the simplest law of motion: a body with no forces acting on it moves in a straight line at a constant speed. The straight line is the problem of space, which is compared or similar to the problem of time. For this law to make a lot of sense, we need to know what it means to move at a constant speed. Time must be factored in. At a constant speed, equal distances are covered in equal times.

One of the most peculiar qualities of time is the fact that it is measured by motion. Time becomes very evident through motion. Sound creates movement and motion. Therefore, the voice of God interjected into our space creates a force on that body that changes the speed of action that is in operation of that body. When God speaks or when man becomes the voice of God and speaks into the environment at a certain point, the atmosphere changes and realigns, and heaven is reflected in the earth realm.

THE HEBREW CONCEPT OF TIME

The Hebrew mind did not think of the passage of time as a medium unto itself like the Greek mind. Our Western civilization views time like the Greeks. Hebrews identified the passage of time as the *life cycle*. The Hebrews saw man as participating in two time dimensions. One "age" of time was temporal—we were placed in nature and interact with the laws of science around us. The other dimension of time was an age to come.

> However, we speak wisdom among those who are mature, yet not the wisdom of this age, nor of the rulers of this age, who are coming to nothing. But we speak the wisdom of God in a mystery, the hidden wisdom which God ordained before the ages for our glory, which none of the rulers of this age knew; for had they known, they would not have crucified the Lord of glory.
>
> —1 CORINTHIANS 2:6–8

Wisdom that God has stored for a time such as this is available to us. We can get to a place of gaining wisdom that no enemy of hell has access to.

From a Hebraic mind-set, events that occurred through life created smaller styles of review of a bigger picture of life. When one summed up all of these smaller temporal cycles, the finite age was determined. However, that did not limit one to just the events of this age. The sum of all the temporal events in one age produced a finite cycle of life. The sum of the events in the age to come was infinite. This was defined as *everlasting*.

In the Hebrew culture, life was defined by events related through relationship. In our culture, we like to *feel time*. We are constantly worried about having *enough time*. To the Hebrew, time was not an object or a thing. Hebrews could not lose time, but they could lose relationship and, therefore, not fully *sum up* the events that should have been equated with their finite life. If you think relationship, you regain the life concept that says that I am important and I am placed here on Earth to accomplish a full purpose. Our attitude should be to stay in relationship and define our life events around relationship until we have fully accomplished all that is being required of us in a relationship. If we don't understand this concept of relationship, then we quit choosing *whom* we will serve each day. Our days are filled with *how* and *what* we will serve. This is what happened in the scenario with Martha and Mary (Luke 10). Mary sat at Jesus's feet and developed a relationship with Him, while Martha was visibly distracted by all that needed to be done. Mary entered into the moment, whereas Martha occupied her day with activity. So, we must be careful how we live, "redeeming the time, because the days are evil" (Eph. 5:16).

God will visit you in time. Be expectant to watch for His coming visitation in your life.

As you read the pages of this book, I will attempt to help you not to fear the days ahead but to develop faith for your future. Life has a process, and many times we get lost in that process because of time and sequences of events. We each go through narrow transitions in life. I hope to help you understand how to relate to a holy God in those narrow transitions and to develop a deep sense of His Spirit guiding you across and into your new destined place.

God will visit you in time. Expectantly watch for His coming visitation in your life. We are a people on the move. God has a kingdom that is within us. The kingdom of God is advancing. We are moving from fellowship into war. We are moving from praise to jubilation as we see a manifestation of His promises in our life cycle.

Issachar was the Israelite tribe that knew how to move into the new. May you decree a new thing and watch it happen. May you understand times and seasons and know what you are to do to succeed in this life. May you see all the blessings in heavenly places that are there for you.

May you overcome every strategy of your enemy, Satan, who changes and manipulates times and laws. May you move past your events of trauma, discouragement, and discontent—events that have created hope deferred and made your heart sick. May you see your horizon line extended and receive an anointing to finish every assignment strong. May you feel God's pleasure in your life NOW!

CHAPTER 2

FEAR NOT! DEVELOPING FAITH
FOR YOUR FUTURE

YOU HAVE, NO DOUBT, HEARD THE PHRASE "NOW IS THE TIME" at numerous junctures in your life. You have probably heard it again and again, and at certain times you may have even quit believing in the word NOW! Or you may have fallen into fear that you were missing the NOW!

I like the story of the blind man beside the road when Jesus was passing.

> Then it happened, as He was coming near Jericho, that a certain blind man sat by the road begging. And hearing a multitude passing by, he asked what it meant. So they told him that Jesus of Nazareth was passing by. And he cried out, saying, "Jesus, Son of David, have mercy on me!" Then those who went before warned him that he should be quiet; but he cried out all the more, "Son of David, have mercy on me!" So Jesus stood still and commanded him to be brought to Him. And when he had come near, He asked him, saying, "What do you want Me to do for you?" And he said, "Lord, that I may receive my sight." Then Jesus said to him, "Receive your sight; your faith has made you well." And immediately he received his sight, and followed Him, glorifying God. And all the people, when they saw it, gave praise to God.
>
> —LUKE 18:35–43

This man was blind and could sense it was his NOW time. What if he had kept silent and not cried out? What if he had listened to his friends and kept quiet? He would have missed his NOW moment and the vision that was waiting for him. His future was released by crying out at the right moment.

The time is now! Revelation 12:10–11 says, "Then I heard a loud voice saying in heaven, 'Now salvation, and strength, and the kingdom of our God, and the power of His Christ have come, for the accuser of our brethren, who accused them before our God day and night, has been cast down. And they overcame him by the blood of the Lamb and by the word of their testimony, and they did not love their lives to the death.'" There is not a word in the Bible that our enemy, the devil, fears more than this word. If we fully embraced this word by the Spirit and with understanding, we would never bow to fear.

The twelfth chapter of Revelation begins with a woman. This woman represents the church standing in full dominion. She is clothed with the sun, the moon is under her feet, and she has a garland of twelve stars around her head. These stars represent the twelve tribes. We will discuss our need prophetically to understand the tribes, their positioning, and their relationship to each of us in chapter 5.

The adversary is represented as a dragon. The dragon has seven heads, ten horns, and seven diadems. The numbers *seven* and *ten* reveal to us complete power and fullness of authority. This also shows us that there is a maturing conflict between the world, the nations, and the church!

The travail of the woman signifies her readiness to give birth. The dragon is waiting to overcome this child. If the dragon is waiting, that means our enemy understands time and knows when to strike. Therefore, the woman must be prepared to flee! Each believer must know when to flee, when to fight, when to stand, and when to overcome! In all of this, we must not be a people of fear.

THIS IS A TIME TO OVERCOME THE SPIRIT OF FEAR

Why fear? With change going on all around us, nations raging against nations, and information technology advancing on a daily basis, we must yield and say, "Lord, teach me!" Teach me to pray, what to say, when to do, and how to maneuver through the chaos of a complex society. If you are willing to change, you will become the head (of the future) and not the tail (wagging from past defeat and falling behind in the understanding of times).

We are living in times when the revolutionaries of the future will arise. They are rising now! These are people filled with discernment and understanding of the times and the activity of the enemy. Even though evil abounds around us, you must be bold! Terrorism, financial instability, increasing litigation, and governmental oppression may be lurking around every corner, but almighty God says you can advance with confidence!

The opposite of boldness is *fear*. Fear can be an emotion and/or a demonic spirit. (See 2 Timothy 1:7.) When you agree with the spirit of fear, you endanger yourself to the possibility of that spirit being embedded in your emotions. This will cause you to grow confused and unstable. The voice of fear says, "There is a lion in my path, and I must hide out." This effectively stops us from advancing.

Fear agrees with a host of other spirits that long to form a net of captivity around you. One of these is the spirit of poverty. This spirit whispers to your soul and says, "God is not able to deal with what I see and hear looming ahead on the path." Fear works with infirmity and weakens your ability to stand. Fear works with control and causes you to react angrily in the midst of change.

> *Terrorism, financial instability, increasing litigation, and governmental oppression may be lurking around every corner, but almighty God says you can advance with confidence!*

HEAVEN AND EARTH ARE REALIGNING

The greatest change in this hour of history is in heavenly places. We are living in interesting times. These days seem like dangerous times, but actually they are times when the Lord is developing His men and women

27

of faith who will rule and take dominion. Heaven and Earth are in a divine realignment. Revelation 12:7–9 (AMP) says:

> Then war broke out in heaven; Michael and his angels went forth to battle with the dragon, and the dragon and his angels fought. But they were defeated, and there was no room found for them in heaven any longer. And the huge dragon was cast down and out—that age-old serpent, who is called the Devil and Satan, he who is the seducer (deceiver) of all humanity the world over; he was forced out and down to the earth, and his angels were flung out along with him.

The obedience of the Lord Jesus Christ to be a sacrifice for mankind secured the triumph over the dragon. However, today we are still engaged in the conflict to enforce the right of dominion that we have been given. The more you pray and cry out to the Lord, the more He pushes the enemy into your sphere of authority in the earth realm. So when the enemy manifests against you or shows up in your path, this is because you are on the verge of winning a great war against him or because you are at a place of birthing your next vision. This is the time that you should shout, "NOW salvation and strength have come!" The manifestation of resisting tactics of the enemy is one of the key road signs that you are walking in victory and entering a NOW season. You have entered into a new time frame, and as verse 12 says, "He knows that his time is short" (NIV).

We are living in a time when the will of heaven is being communicated to God's prophets and apostles of this age. This is releasing an *overpowering* strength in His people. This is causing the headship of the god of this world to be subdued.

God is realigning the sounds of heaven in the earth. This is changing the way the church has *worshiped* individually and corporately! Our time and days are being *reordered*. We are learning to worship and watch in new ways. I recently wrote a book called *Reordering Your Day: Understanding and Embracing the Four Prayer Watches*.[1] This book explains all four prayer watches and how the Lord ordained evening before morning and called us to watch one hour with Him. When we move with Him to watch and pray, He reorders our day. This is resulting in the tabernacle of David being restored for this generation! Amos 9:11–12 says, "On that day I will raise up the tabernacle of David, which has fallen down, and repair its damages; I will raise up its ruins, and rebuild it as in the days of old; that they may possess the remnant of Edom, and all the Gentiles who are called by My name." When we are at the right place at the right time, then we are assured of success and victory.

In every generation, God has a plan to restore the tabernacle of David. The prophecy above is also quoted in Acts 15. This prophecy and promise is passed on from generation to generation. It's necessary to see restoration of the areas that David installed in worship to see the fullness of the Gentiles come in to the kingdom of God. James was saying that as they built the church for the generations to come, they would include the process of the restoration of David's tabernacle so that the Gentiles would know the Lord.

In *The Worship Warrior*, John Dickson and I write:

> Probably more people know more about King David than any biblical character other than Jesus. He was a shepherd. He was a musician. He was a composer. He was a national civil hero. He was a prophet. He was a king. He was a warrior. He also received divine revelation for the temple that his son, Solomon, would build. God provided him the blueprint, which he passed on to Solomon. From this blueprint, once the temple was completed, the glory of God filled every crevice (1 Kings 8:10–15). Whereas the tabernacle of Moses was for the Israelites alone, the tabernacle of David included both Jew and Gentile.
>
> 1. David's tabernacle pointed us toward a new covenant filled with grace and faith.
>
> 2. David's tabernacle pointed us to a new church order, where all believers could be kings and priests. David demonstrated this.

3. David's tabernacle, after the dedication, shifted from animal sacrifices to sacrifices of joy, thanksgiving, and praise.

4. David's tabernacle became the habitation of the ark of God's presence until the temple was completed.

5. David's tabernacle had the ark of the covenant and foretold of someone who would come and sit upon the throne forever.

6. David's tabernacle didn't have a veil, so there was access. This represented mediation and intercession.

7. David's tabernacle had singers, musical instruments, and songs of praise within the confines of the tent. A new order and continual sound of worship arose.

8. David's tabernacle opened the door for the coming of all nations. Whether you were circumcised or uncircumcised, you had access to this tabernacle.

When God says He is restoring the tabernacle of David, He is not bringing us to an Old Testament order. He is just making sure that everything is shifted from the law of Moses's tabernacle to the prophetic life-giving power that we find in David's tabernacle. The heavenly pattern that we see now that God is leading us into is found all through the Book of Revelation. I believe if we will worship, we will see all that David demonstrated for us, his passion to establish God's presence and to rule as a warrior over his enemies from that presence, being restored to us individually and corporately.[2]

Do you really believe that your life can make a difference if you are at the right place at the right time? *Relentless Generational Blessings* by Arthur Burk is a very interesting book that reveals how God intends each of us to have a generational impact in this world.[3] This very positive book encourages us to see generational blessings in our families as opposed to the negative traits and failures that seem to derail success. This book discusses how we not only inherit a toxic waste dump we do not deserve (our generational curses), but we also inherit a gold mine that we have not earned (our generational blessings). You should recog-

nize your life this way. You should also recognize that each state that makes up this nation has incredible blessings in the midst of strife and defilement, and each generation has a responsibility to bring forth those blessings. That is why we are on the earth.

I always define *success* as being at the right place at the right time doing the right thing. That is what we actually tried to do on the Fifty-State Tour when Dutch Sheets and I traveled together to minister in all fifty states. We tried to be in each state at the right time and

The realignment of heaven and earth is moving you from conformity to transformation.

decree what God was saying so that the people in that state could move forward in God's perfect will.

There is a supernatural realignment of the generations! Isaiah 59:21 (AMP) says:

> As for Me, this is My covenant or league with them, says the Lord: My Spirit, Who is upon you [and Who writes the law of God inwardly on the heart], and My words which I have put in your mouth shall not depart out of your mouth, or out of the mouths of your [true, spiritual] children, or out of the mouths of your children's children, says the Lord, from henceforth and forever.

When the generations begin to prophesy and speak forth the same thing, then you see heaven, the earth, and the future realigned. When three generations say the same thing, hell can do nothing but tremble.

The realignment of heaven and earth is moving you from *conformity* to *transformation*. When the revelation of heaven confronts your mind with truth and revelation, do not hesitate to embrace change! Fear not because of your past! Your past will submit to your future! Time cannot hold you captured in the past—the best is still ahead for you.

THE PHRASES OF TIME

Even while I am writing this book, I realize how much we use the word *time* in our sentences and speech. Needless to say, I think we are preoccupied and our lives revolve around *time*. Here are some more key phrases we use about time:

- "Keep me abreast of the times."
- "I am working against time."
- "I am running ahead of time."
- "At one time, this situation occurred."
- "At the same time, several situations were working."
- "That group is behind the times."
- "I have fallen behind time on my schedule."
- "I am between times of waiting."
- "For the time being, this is how I will approach this situation."
- "From time to time I get a card or a call."
- "I need to gain time on my opponent."
- "In good time you will see results."
- "In no time and no way will I do that."
- "Go, and do not lose time."
- "Make time, and make money too."
- "On one's own time…"
- "I am out of time."
- "I am just trying to pass the time of day."

- "Time after time…"

- "This is the time of my life."

In *God's Timing for Your Life*, Dutch Sheets shares the following:

The word *chronos* refers to the general process of time or chronological time. The word *kairos* refers to the right time, the opportune
or strategic time, the now time. As I was doing this [studying these
two words for time], God began to reveal a very important truth
to me. I have always completely separated these two concepts—
chronological time and the right time—but God has been showing
me that this is not accurate. Often, they are simply different phases
of the same process. *Kairos*, in many ways, is an extension or
continuation of *chronos*. As the processes of God's plans unfold,
chronos becomes *kairos*. The new is connected to the old and, in
fact, is often the result of what happened in the old. *Kairos*, the
opportune time, is literally born of *chronos*, the general time. When
we're in a nonstrategic general season of life's daily routine, plod-
ding along in the *chronos* time, God doesn't totally start over with a
kairos season. His overall agenda does not change. He simply takes
us through one phase of a process in which our perseverance and
faithfulness have allowed Him to shift us into the next phase—a
strategic season. He changes the time and season, transforming
chronos into *kairos*.[4]

FEAR NOT YOUR NARROW, TIGHT PLACES!

Recently I heard the Lord say the following:

Do not be afraid to walk that high wire that I have put you on.
I have stretched the wire tight, and it will not lag. If you will walk
across the place that seems too high and deep, I will extend My
hand, steady your walk, and get you to the other side. Not only
should you walk on the high wire, but dance, and you will begin to
overthrow that which has been ruling you in the heavens. Do not be

afraid to dance in the high place. Dance across that place that looks deep and ominous, and this will be known as your "leap of faith." You will enter into a realm of boldness and confidence that you have never known. *Do not look down, and do not look back.* Keep your head up, for your redemption is drawing nigh. Look forward. I am calling you to stand on a new platform and in a new place. There is a sound of drawing and there is a sound of purifying, for this is a time when I am drawing My people to Me. I am preparing you for that place where you will stand, and stand uncompromisingly. You will begin to move near Me. Feel and sense My fragrance in a way you've never sensed Me before. You will become a fragrance in the earth realm, and where death is working, you will begin to create a new smell. Come forth! In the midst of the decay of your past, I will cause fallow ground to be broken up and flowers to bloom. Draw near, and you will blossom this hour.

While I was speaking this word, my thought was, "So many are afraid of heights. Being on a tightrope or connecting and walking through a narrow place creates anxiety." Linda Heidler shared the following after I released the word:

When I used to go to Pioneer Girls camp with Lindy, they had a high ropes course. It went about forty feet up into the trees. Before you started up, they strapped you into a harness so that you could not fall. The first part of the course was to climb a giant web of rope up to the first platform. From there you walked across a series of tightropes, each one taking you higher. Each level had a different kind of support rope for you to hold on to. There were small platforms between the levels of ropes. If you kept your focus on the next platform, it was very easy to walk across the rope. If you looked at your feet or the ground, you would lose your balance. If you looked back, your feet would miss the rope as you tried to take your next step forward. There were people to assist you at each platform who would give you instructions and encourage you to just keep moving and to not look down. If you kept focused on them and followed their instructions, it was really fun to keep going higher.

We will share many issues in a chapter ahead about the dangerous snares of the narrow transitions of our lives.

FEAR NOT!

Throughout the Word of God, we find these two words: "Fear not." Fear is a powerful, unpleasant feeling associated with risk or danger. This emotion can be real or imagined. The emotion of fear is a defensive response to a stimulus that has entered the atmosphere around us. This emotion serves as a motivation to escape to a place of safety. Fear is a feeling of agitation and anxiety caused by the presence of danger. Fear can become a way of life if you anxiously anticipate all kinds of dangers that could overtake you. Fear that is integrated into your reasoning faculties can produce great confusion in your life. Second Timothy 1:7 says, "For God has not given us a spirit of fear, but of power and of love and of a sound mind."

Fear can torment an individual and make that person feel powerless, paralyzed, and alone. Fear comes in many shapes and forms. Fear causes an alertness to arise within your soul. This is a wonderful emotion if it is under the control of the Holy Spirit. If not, the spirit of fear begins to control you and vex your spirit man, with a resulting loss in power as well as demonic infiltration.

Fear has a progression that leads to a downward spiral. Once one fear begins, that fear connects with countless scenarios that lead you into captivity—producing a lack of joy and a loss of peace.

Here is an example. The fear of falling causes you constantly to be unsure of the steps you are taking. If you begin to fall, another fear, that of injury, comes upon you. The fear of abandonment is initiated because you are never sure anyone will be there to catch you. In your fear of injury, you develop anxiety over how you will be injured and who will take care of you. You then have a fear of the future, over how your supply and provision will come. Fear leads to despair and desolation, and eventually your faith is completely overcome and undone.

Fear can be one of the most addicting of all emotions because of the adrenaline rush and chemical flood that occurs in your body. However, in welcoming repeated adrenaline rushes, you grow unaware of the stress that this spirit produces on your organs. Eventually, fear can be like a drug that you must have in order to live and to cope with the changing society around you.

Fear is based on something that you think *may* happen in the future. When you create scenarios in your mind that do not come from hearing the voice of God, the grinding mental process that occurs within you causes a friction in your soul, which eventually results in many physical weaknesses and infirmities. Conversely, prophecy prepares you for the future, because the voice of God produces faith. *Fear is the opposite of love and negates the working of faith.* Fear is a projection of your mind and reasoning that brings you into enmity with the God who created you and sent His Son to redeem you, giving you eternal victory over death. The greatest of fears seems to be the fear of death. Hebrews 2:14–15 says that when your love is pure, all spirits of fear are bound from operating within your soul.

One of the greatest fears known to man is fear of the dark. When the time came for the Lord to liberate His people and press them out of bondage and into their promise, He sent a plague of darkness upon those holding them in bondage. In the plague of darkness, God demonstrated His power over the sun. The sun was Egypt's greatest symbol of worship. Pharaoh was considered the incarnation of the sun god Ra. Therefore, this plague showed that the one true God, Jehovah, had power over light and was Himself light! This demonstration of the Lord's power brought great confusion to the world system of that day. For those aligned with darkness, this brought great fear. However, those who trusted in God were secure.

Fear is the opposite of love and negates the working of faith.

LET FEAR WORK TO YOUR ADVANTAGE

Fear can work with your intuition to help in the process of guarding and protecting your life and what belongs to you. When you get a *feeling of fear*, that can be a form of discernment allowing you to know that something isn't right in your environment. I believe that if you develop your prophetic and predictive skills in the Spirit, fear can turn into great insight. If you deny the emotion of fear, you can lose sight of danger around you. Similarly, if the emotion of fear is not brought under the power of the Spirit of God, a spirit of fear will take advantage of the emotion and control you so you fail in making sound decisions.

One benefit of fear is that the emotion you sense can predict what might be coming down your road. However, you must never fall to panic. Panic occurs when your imagination takes control of the sense you are perceiving in your emotions. When you receive a fear signal in your emotions, you must be careful to analyze what that signal links to.

When the concept of fear is studied and analyzed, you find that many surveys rank the fear of death and the fear of public speaking as number one and two respectively. In the fear of death, we are afraid that we will lose our last breath. And because many of us have never experienced a vision of eternity, we are really not sure what will happen after that last breath has been breathed. In the fear of public speaking, we are afraid that if we fail in what we are trying to communicate, people will not perceive the identity of who we really are.

You must learn to manage emotions that are emitted from the inward part of your being. Then you can prepare yourself for the future and even predict what will be coming in days ahead. Fear causes you to think on what might happen. Stop thinking about all the fictional scenarios that could happen, and instead respond by faith so that the powerful emotion of fear does not stop you dead in your tracks.

There are other benefits of fear. The reverential fear that there is Someone greater than us whom we can worship and adore leads to wisdom and action. When you receive warnings by the Holy Spirit, you become alert in dangerous situations. This causes you to even walk through minefields with confidence. As you rely upon the power of God and His revealed purpose in your life, you will receive grace to overcome any strategy of hell that has entered your atmosphere. To develop your true identity, you must overcome fear. (See Isaiah 41.) Your identity in the Lord gives you authority.

Stop thinking about all the fictional scenarios that could happen, and instead respond by faith so that the powerful emotion of fear does not stop you dead in your tracks.

The Lord is sending a heavenly sword to you in the midst of the confusion of the world around you! This sword of His Word will give you confidence and equip you to *cut through* into the next stage of your life. As God's people, we need to be filled with new strength and joy. We need to learn to laugh at our enemies and the confusion around us. As we experience a sense of laughter, abounding joy, and the power of barrenness and drought being broken from our spheres of authority, we should wear a garment of praise for the principalities and powers to see. Begin to change your spiritual wardrobe to put on garments of confidence, strength, joy, and praise.

With these spiritual garments in place, you can have the same effect on the people around you as the spies Joshua sent to spy out Jericho had on the Canaanites, who fearfully awaited the Israelites' taking of the Promised Land. In Joshua 2, Rahab told the spies: "As soon as we heard these things [the testimony of the Red Sea crossing forty years earlier], our hearts melted; neither did there remain any more courage in anyone because of you" (v. 11).

We are dangerous creatures with great authority in the earth realm. When we are filled with God we should not fear, but we should proceed with confidence into the destiny that He planned for us before the foundation of the earth. This is a time in which we need to exercise boldness.

There is a great advantage that light has over darkness. The Holy Spirit is a witness to the light and gives revelation on breaking the power of darkness around us. Therefore you do not need to be afraid of the dark!

Decree that any curse that has been spoken and set against you will be overturned. Declare that the bitter will become sweet. Shout, "My fear shall laugh!" Declare deliverance from any deep hidden grief. Ask the Lord for joy and laughter to arise in your emotions. Declare that your emotions will be healed and restored. Ask the Lord to increase your faith so fear is overcome. When God enters time and speaks to you, faith enters your environment and atmosphere, and fear must flee!

What Faith Is

Our faith is more precious than gold (1 Pet. 1:7). Faith is the central concept of Christianity. To be called a *Christian* means you are one who places your faith and trust in Jesus Christ of Nazareth. One of the greatest pieces of our Christian armor is the shield of faith. If you are going to understand what your shield of faith is and how to protect yourself from your enemies, you need to understand what the shield is made of. Faith is related to every aspect of your life. As a child of God, how you process faith in time is an important key to overcoming the conformity of the world around you.

By faith we receive salvation (Eph. 2:8–9). Our experiences of sanctification (Acts 26:18), purification (Acts 15:9), justification (Rom. 4:5; 5:1), and adoption (Gal. 3:26; Col. 3:24) are all dependent upon our faith. Faith was the main teaching of Jesus's ministry. In the Gospels, we continually find statements such as, "Your *faith* has healed you." In Jesus's hometown, He could not do mighty miracles because the people there lacked faith. He wasn't powerless to do so, but the atmosphere in that place prevented our Lord from exhibiting the power of faith. However, whenever He found men and women of faith, He released His power, and miracles took place. God assures us that *if we believe*, then nothing is impossible, and He withholds nothing.

In *Restoring Your Shield of Faith*, Robert Heidler and I write:

> The Bible teaches that if we can *get in* faith and *stay in* faith, everything else will come. (See Matthew 8:13; 15:28; Mark 9:23.) I don't

care what needs we face in our life, if we can move into a position of faith and stay there, we will walk in victory on a day-to-day basis. The Greek word for faith is *pistis*. It means to have trust or confidence. When we walk in faith, we are trusting and showing confidence in God in the midst of our situation. Jesus' call to "have faith in God" (Mark 11:22) was an exhortation to enter into a trusting commitment to the Father in the midst of whatever we might face. When Jesus said, "Your faith has made you whole," He was teaching that *confidence in* or *allegiance to* God releases God's wholeness into our lives.[5]

Faith is a fruit of the Holy Spirit (Gal. 5:22–23). There is also a spiritual gift of faith (1 Cor. 12:8–9). In times of need, the Holy Spirit can release to you a greater measure of faith. However, unless your shield of faith is in place, you cannot see all of these dimensions of faith activated. Therefore, when your spirit man interacts by the Holy Spirit with Father God through Jesus Christ, God, who is not in time, moves in time in us! The interaction of God and man in time produces fruit.

> Now faith is the assurance (the confirmation, the title deed) of the things [we] hope for, being the proof of things [we] do not see and the conviction of their reality [faith perceiving as real fact what is not revealed to the senses].
>
> —HEBREWS 11:1, AMP

R. T. Kendall gives wonderful insight into this aspect of faith:

> Faith is that which keeps us looking beyond what we can see with our natural senses, with such confidence that we know we shall not be disappointed. Faith looks beyond oneself, never within oneself. Faith always leads us outside ourselves. Why? Because faith perceives its object—God. The main insight the writer's statement conveys, however, is what faith is *not*. It is the "evidence of things not seen." The Greek is *pragmaton elegchos ou blepomenon*— literally, "persuasion of the works not seen." One is convinced that one will see them; one is truly persuaded that one will see them. But

one does not see them at the moment. Therefore, faith is not *seeing* the tangible. If one sees now what one previously had been waiting for, it ceases to be called faith. Until what someone was waiting for literally appears, such waiting is graced with the title *faith*.[6]

LET FAITH ARISE!

When talking about faith and time and how they work together, one of my favorite scriptures is Hebrews 11:23 (AMP):

> [Prompted] by faith Moses, after his birth, was kept concealed for three months by his parents, because they saw how comely the child was; and they were not overawed and terrified by the king's decree.

Moses's parents had three months of faith!

This is a time for faith to arise in the midst of the curses that would try to rob you of your future. Know that your deliverance is forming. In Exodus 1, we find that Pharaoh had an anti-Semitic heart. His goal was to destroy all of Israel by removing the male children who would be the future leaders of Israel. His decree that every newborn son be cast into the

Distrust is projected fear. Trusting in God is one way that you overthrow a curse.

river resulted in a death curse on the wombs of the Hebrew mothers. The astrologers of Egypt thought that the deliverer of the Jewish people would suffer misfortune through water.[7] That is why I believe Pharaoh decided to have all the newborn boys thrown into the water.

Moses was God's prophetic choice to redeem Israel. His mother *redeemed this death curse by trusting God* and placing her son in the water. Distrust is projected fear. Trusting in God is one way that you can overthrow a curse. A key to Moses's life was that he was ordained as a prophet from birth. Even though his insecurity would tell him he could not speak, God had ordained him as a prophet. The faith of Moses's mother and father, which worked through love for their son, would eventually result in the deliverance of all of Israel. This faith would also give

Moses authority to split the sea for the escape of God's people. Moses would also receive the Law, which would set the commandments and boundaries for mankind.

There are new boundaries for you to obtain this season. Let the prophetic gift arise in you. Let a new level of deliverance begin. Now is a time to:

1. Declare that any root of depression and despair break. I suggest a fruit and vegetable diet for three days.

2. Bind any confused communication or miscommunication. Declare that your words and expressions will be clear.

3. Ask the Lord to remove your worry and anxiety over supply. This is a time to overturn worry through the release of supply. Declare that you will find your supply in "hidden" dimensions.

4. Ask the Lord to give you the measure of faith you need to enable you to do the *next thing* He requires of you.

Three months' worth of faith can save a whole nation and people! The faith action of one time frame can manifest greatly in another time frame. The faith of Moses's mother paid off eighty years later when God appeared to her son in a burning bush and commissioned him to deliver His people from Egypt.

FEAR OF THE FUTURE

One of the greatest faith robbers of life is the *fear of the future*. The prophetic gift is very important in building faith and hope. One of my favorite stories is in the Book of Jeremiah when God told him to buy the field at Anathoth. (See Jeremiah 32:7–9.) Jeremiah was imprisoned for prophesying that drastic change would come to Jerusalem. God then comes to him while he is in prison and tells him to buy a field. This field is one of the fields that he had prophesied would be destroyed over the next seventy years. In this, I believe the Lord was attempting to show Jeremiah not to fear the future. There will always be a plan for the remnant in days ahead. If you will watch and listen, then you will hear God in your troubling circumstances. He will give you a picture of the future.

Like Jeremiah, we must be willing to obey God in these troubling times. Even if He asks us to do something unusual, we must remember that God has plans and purposes far beyond what we are able to see or comprehend—plans for good and not evil, plans for a hope and a future (Jer. 29:11).

When God enters time and speaks to you, faith enters your environment and atmosphere, and fear must flee!

The coming days will be likened to those of Moses in which demonstrations of God's power will overthrow today's pharaohs in order to bring about the redemption of entire territories. Numbers 33:3–4 holds a key principle for the days ahead: "The children of Israel went out with boldness in the sight of all the Egyptians. For the Egyptians were burying all their firstborn, whom the LORD had killed among them. Also on their gods the LORD had executed judgments." The Egyptians were burying their dead since their gods had been rendered powerless; they could not stop the Israelites from leaving. God always has a path of freedom. When your present captivity attempts to overcome you, know that there is a way of escape.

CATCH THE ROPE OF HOPE

Future is linked with hope. The Hebrew word *tiqvah*, or hope, signifies a cord that you can grab hold of so that you can have an expected outcome.[8] I always watch for my *rope of hope* that is being extended from heaven. I know that God's outcome for any trying situation that I am in is better than I can even imagine. Jeremiah 31:17 says, "And there is hope for your future, says the Lord; your children shall come back to their own country" (AMP). In the midst of captivity, God kept prophesying through Jeremiah so that His covenant people would not lose their expectation of Him.

We must never lose our hope for deliverance. This is part of the ground that we stand on. Hope is linked with watching for an expected outcome to manifest.

> The fear of the LORD prolongs days, but the years of the wicked will be shortened. The hope of the righteous will be gladness, but the expectation of the wicked will perish. The way of the LORD is strength for the upright, but destruction will come to the workers of iniquity.
>
> —PROVERBS 10:27–29

God's people must never lose their expectation of Him. If we do, our wounded emotions will become filled with fear. Trauma will be more fully explained in the next book in this series on redeeming time. However, I do want to say that when we experience trauma, the memory of the trauma imbeds within our cell structure. Trauma always competes with hope to remove our faith level in a holy God who can restore us.

The ground we stand on must be filled with hope. In Proverbs 10:30–31, we read: "The righteous will never be removed, but the wicked will not inhabit the earth. The mouth of the righteous brings forth wisdom." I have learned to watch. We must always remember to lift our head, for our redemption is coming to us. If you will keep your head up, your eyes will see the *rope of hope* being extended from heaven.

> Therefore, behold, I will allure her,
> Will bring her into the wilderness,
> And speak comfort to her.
> I will give her her vineyards from there,
> And the Valley of Achor as a *door of hope*;
> She shall sing there,
> As in the days of her youth,
> As in the day when she came up from the land of Egypt.
>
> —HOSEA 2:14–15, emphasis added

When you are in wilderness times, you must remember that a door in heaven will open. This door is filled with hope. Imagine from that door a rope being extended that will pull you up and out of any pit that is trying to overtake you. Another way of looking at this is the door of heaven will open, a rope will come down, you will grab hold, all fear and unbelief will leave your emotions, and you will stand strong in the midst of your trial. This will give you the future or expected end that God has planned for you to reach.

GO UP AND BREAK THROUGH

The Breaker [the Messiah] will go up before them. They will break through, pass in through the gate and go out through it, and their King will pass on before them, the Lord at their head.

—MICAH 2:13, AMP

The breaker anointing is the anointing that is received when we understand that the Anointed One, the Messiah, has gone before us and broken the headship of our enemy. Those with the breaker anointing are those who walk in the ministry of a forerunner.

The breaker anointing will break fear away from you as you move into the future. To have an overcoming spirit, you must come to a place of intimacy and deep communion with God. This causes what God is trying to birth on the earth to be conceived deep within you. Overcoming Christians understand travail. (We will discuss travail in the next chapter.) Once something has been conceived in them, they know they must travail until it has been birthed. This is not a time of fear but rather a time of overcoming and birthing. A person with an overcoming spirit produces breakthrough. God is releasing an overcoming anointing for spiritual breakthrough.

In *The Breaker Anointing*, Barbara Yoder writes that the breaker anointing "affects individuals, churches and cities. When the breaker anointing comes into an area, it results in changes not only in individuals, churches and the socio-political structure and belief systems of the city.... To accomplish this mission [of transformation], this breed of radical shakers and movers needs a new anointing: an anointing that will break through every obstacle to further the spread of the gospel and to bring about the salvation of individuals and territories to the uttermost.... The breaker anointing is the anointing that breaks us through every *kairos* (opportune) challenge."[9]

The Christian believer is confident of the future because he belongs to Jesus Christ.

The future is a fuel that greatly propels human fear. Not knowing what will happen can produce paralyzing effects in those prone to such fear. On the other hand, the future is also linked with expectations, anticipation, or hope for an occurrence, like the birth of a child. These expectations can cause us to have a passion, joy, strength, and faith in what God will do.

WHY THE FUTURE CAN MAKE US NERVOUS

The word *future* connotes "a time that is yet to come" (Ps. 37:37–38). After the archangel Gabriel interpreted Daniel's vision, he said to Daniel, "Seal up the vision, for it refers to many days in the future" (Dan. 8:26). Because we belong to Christ, we are very confident of the future. We have a hope. We are not afraid to declare the hope that is within us. The Christian believer is confident of the future because he belongs to Jesus Christ.

Acharon is a Hebrew word that is linked with space and time. Basically, it means, "at the back."[10] When we study the account of Jacob returning to Canaan, we see that as he traveled, he put the handmaids and their children first, Leah and her children next, and Rachel and Joseph last (Gen. 33:2). In Jacob's heart, Joseph was the future, or the one who would inherit the double portion. When journeying back to the Promised Land from Laban's land, he put the most important last. This is a wonderful concept of future. Future is linked with the generation that is to come.

The combination of "first" and "last" creates a concept of completeness. This combination also expresses the sufficiency of the Lord, since He is said to include within Himself the beginning of things, and He is waiting for the completion of something to occur in the end. This is what makes Him *Alpha*, "first," as well as *Omega*, "last." Isaiah 44:6 states, "Thus says the LORD, the King of Israel, and his Redeemer, the LORD of hosts: 'I am the First and I am the Last; besides Me there is no God.'" A great concept of future is this: "I will not delay to get you to the best place of finishing that I have for you!"

However, delays and the finite time frame that encompasses our vision create anxiety in our lives. Many times we do not keep a heavenly perspective, and we cannot see the end from the beginning. Consequently, we tend to become anxious in the middle, and fear overwhelms us.

EIGHT KEY PARADIGM EVALUATIONS FOR DETERMINING YOUR FUTURE

We often forget that Jesus had only three years to teach a group of chosen men what He was about and what Father was doing so that they would be prepared for the future. Sometimes I think one woman, Mary Magdalene, understood Him better than the others.

One of my favorite passages in Jesus's teaching is Luke 14:25–35. This passage has changed my life. Major crowds were following Jesus because of the miracles He performed. Jesus uses this passage to define discipleship to His followers, including the twelve chosen disciples who were with Him. A *disciple* is one who is teachable and is being taught. Any time you are unwilling to be taught or you become unteachable, your progress ends, and you are not prepared for the future.

In this passage, the Lord is sharing that if anyone comes to Him, then they must leave all other attachments and commitments. It seems a very hard statement—you must leave father, mother, wife, children, brothers, and sisters, and even your own life to be taught by Him (v. 25). I believe this passage is saying this: "If you are going to learn from Me, then you are going to have to make Me preeminent in your life. You cannot have an emotional attachment to something or someone that is greater than your devotion to Me. If you do, then you won't be able to receive what I am trying to provide so you can advance into your future and represent Me in days ahead."

He then goes on to share two major principles that He was teaching His disciples. One was about war, the other about building. When I was reading this passage the Lord gave me the following eight questions to meditate upon. I believe these will be a tremendous help to determine if you are prepared to move forward in days ahead.

1. *How are you building for the future?* What revelation got you started in your building process? What emotions have hindered you?

2. *If you are in a leadership position, how are you choosing your leadership?* Is your mantle transferable? How are you building and aligning with the next generation?

3. *Are you developing a strategy for reviewing assignments and expansion limits?* How do you plan to increase and multiply?

4. *Do you have an increase strategy?* Are you just maintaining on a day-to-day basis? Have you done a market analysis? What do you have to work with? How can you optimize your resources?

5. *What is your strategy of giving?* Is there a more legitimate righteous structure that you are giving into? Giving is the principle of heaven that unlocks your future.

6. *Have you evaluated your shield of protection, account-ability, and submission structure?* Whom are you aligned with? Who has apostolic authority in your sphere of influence? Who is speaking into your life? What authority structures are part of your life? No greater faith had Jesus

seen in all of Israel than the man who understood authority (Matt. 8:5–13).

7. *Have you gotten "the council in position"?* Who is seated in the council with you concerning your assignment and sphere? Are you seated in a place of influence? Who influences you? Who can give you the input to arrange your puzzle so you see the full vision that is there for you in days ahead? Your provision is linked with your vision.

8. *Do you understand and are you capable of resisting the warfare in your sphere?* If you are in business, have you looked for patterns of covenant breaking, bloodshed, idolatry, and immorality? Have you applied this to each territory that you are attempting to enter? If you are in ministry, what would stop your growth, rob your favor, and block your influence?

PREPARE FOR THE FUTURE

Expect the Lord to meet you at every turn. Bask in His presence. Let Him prepare you for the days ahead. Do not walk in anxiety and fear, but be filled with faith. In *The Future War of the Church*, Rebecca Wagner Sytsema and I wrote on the importance of preparation. We seem to always be crossing over or going from one transition to another.

> Transition is a time of preparation. During this time of transition for the Church, God is preparing His people to be victorious in the days ahead. When considering a Scripture passage or a word of prophecy, I find it helpful to open the dictionary and review the definitions of key words in order to fully understand what the Lord may want to reveal.
>
> According to the word I received, in this hour God is preparing the Church for war. The key words to understand are "prepare," "Church" and "war." Let us first look at the word "prepare." To *prepare* means to make ready or get ready, to put together or

compound, to formulate, to draft, to draw up, to frame, to ready for action, to gird, to brace, to fortify or to strengthen. God believes strongly in preparation. In fact, the word "prepare" appears in nearly every book of the Old Testament. We are to be a people prepared to do that which God has called us to do.[11]

Preparation is a word that involves time. There are many kinds of actions linked to preparing for Your future. You must qualify for a particular purpose or end. Sometimes this requires a four-year curriculum of study that results in certification or receiving a diploma. To plant seed for a future crop, you must prepare the soil by tilling the ground. To develop a beautiful garment, you must prepare the cloth that is necessary to create what you will wear in days ahead. As we instruct those around us who are following in our footsteps, we prepare them by educating or teaching them certain methods. If you are going to have an elegant dinner for a group of people, then you must prepare the meal and the table.

Do not grow weary in your preparation stages of life.

In war, you must prepare a ship and fill it with arms, ammunition, and provisions for the troops. If you do not prepare this ship, then you will find yourself *needy* in defense against your enemies. You must even prepare your heart so that it can be filled with happiness and joy. The Bible says in Amos 4:12, "Prepare to meet your God." The Lord has prepared His throne in the heavens. He is guiding, directing, and establishing us, making all things suitable by His order so that we are victorious in every situation. Do not grow weary in your preparation stages of life.

The Ten Virgins: Will You Be Surprised by God or Unprepared to Meet Him?

There are so many situational teachings that Jesus did on preparation that could help us. However, the one that I feel is very pertinent for today is the parable of the ten virgins. The setting is the Mount of Olives. The parable is about the end of the age and the coming of the kingdom of heaven. We are in a similar time now in the earth realm. The kingdom of God is compared to the procession of the wedding. In this wedding are ten virgins who go out to meet the bridegroom. Some take oil, and some do not. You can read the story in Matthew 25:1–13. This parable can be summarized as follows:

> Be ye personally prepared; be ye prepared for any length of time; be ye prepared to go to Him directly....Each guest may, indeed, come to the banqueting-hall, but the final judgment as to his worthiness belongs to God....to partake of the feast requires personal and individual preparation...the main lessons of the Parable are the need of individual, personal, and spiritual preparation.[12]

Only our discipline and preparation will enable us to endure the trials of the world and age we live in as we wait for the ultimate coming of Christ in His fullness. There is a *procession* occurring today. The ark of His presence is moving through the earth. Many of us are waiting patiently to see Him move and unlock the blessings He has for this age. We must run to this procession and be prepared to wait until we see the door of opportunity positioned before us. Then we must not hesitate but move quickly into our position for the future. We must always be prepared for visitation and a summons to meet with our Lord. Alfred Edersheim says:

> The first point which we mark is that the Ten Virgins brought presumably to the bridal house, "their own" lamps. Emphasis must be laid on this. Thus much was there of personal preparation on the part of all....All of them have brought their own lamps....But only the wise have more than this—the oil in the vessels, without which the lamps cannot give their light. "Let your light shine..." (Matt. 5:16). They [foolish virgins] brought their own lamps but not oil. The foolishness of the five Virgins therefore consisted, not...*in their want of perseverance*—as if the oil had been consumed before the Bridegroom

came, and they had only not provided themselves with a sufficient extra-supply—*but in the entire absence of personal preparation.*[13]

The church, the *One New Man* that is forming and coming into fullness, is being prepared to be the bridal companion of Christ. We will participate in the wedding feast. We will be surprised, disappointed, and very confused "if we neglect the preparation of grace, personal conversation and holiness, trusting that in the hour of need the oil may be supplied out of the common stock. But they know not, or else heed not, that every one must be personally prepared for meeting the Bridegroom, that the call will be sudden, that the stock of oil is not common, and that the time between His arrival and the shutting of the door will be awfully brief."[14]

Here are some key principles from this parable:

1. The supply "must be their own."

2. There is a major difference between being surprised and being unprepared when visitation comes. Both sets of virgins were surprised, but one group was caught unprepared.

3. We cannot make up for the neglect of previous preparation.

4. We can be excluded and treated as strangers to the Bridegroom.

5. Joy comes when we have made ourselves ready. We are healthy in our emotions when we wait with expectancy. Revelation 19:7 says, "Let us be glad and rejoice and give Him glory, for the marriage of the Lamb has come, and His wife has made herself ready."

A TIME TO SECURE YOUR FUTURE

One of my favorite stories in the Bible is that of Naomi and Ruth. I have written, taught, and prophesied from the Book of Ruth on numerous occasions. They were two women in covenant relationship. Naomi had lost her inheritance. Ruth had lost her husband, and in that day, that was her future. Their past and present were so lacking that they decided to move forward—not knowing what future was ahead.

Chapter 3 of the Book of Ruth is the turning or "tipping point" chapter. The events in this chapter are rich in teaching time shifts. In verses 1–4, we find:

> Then Naomi her mother-in-law said to her, "My daughter, shall I not seek security for you, that it may be well with you? Now Boaz, whose young women you were with, is he not our relative? In fact, he is winnowing barley tonight at the threshing floor. Therefore wash yourself and anoint yourself, put on your best garment and go down to the threshing floor; but do not make yourself known to the man until he has finished eating and drinking. Then it shall be, when he lies down, that you shall notice the place where he lies; and you shall go in, uncover his feet, and lie down; and he will tell you what you should do."

Notice that Naomi perceives that after gleaning for a complete harvest season, there needs to be a shift. She has a plan to secure their future! This plan starts by remembering the law of inheritance that she had learned as a child, returning to that law, and then developing a plan for redeeming the past and present and entering into the future. I love what Naomi said: "Shall I not seek security [or secure your future] for you?"

To *secure* is to guard effectively from danger by fortifying something so it is beyond hazard.[15] This can happen by us confining, building a hedge, and making certain that no enemy can enter our boundaries. We are not living in a world without danger, but we are living in times when we can feel secure. The Spirit of the Lord can transform your mind so you are free from fear and apprehension. He has a wonderful future for you. Do not fear what is ahead! The Lord assures us:

> For I know the thoughts that I think toward you, says the LORD, thoughts of peace and not of evil, to give you a future and a hope.
>
> —JEREMIAH 29:11

There is hope in your future, says the LORD,
That your children shall come back to their own border.

—JEREMIAH 31:17

Mark the blameless man, and observe the upright;
For the future of that man is peace.
But the transgressors shall be destroyed together;
The future of the wicked shall be cut off.

—PSALM 37:37–38

Let me paraphrase what Naomi was saying: "TONIGHT is our NOW, Ruth! Get cleaned up, look good, get rid of that widow's garment that you have worn for a year, get anointed, and go to where the celebration is! When you get there, wait until midnight, and then when Boaz is asleep, lie down and submit yourself to him. If you will do this, our future will be secured! Tonight is our future!" The rest is history. Ruth's obedience secured my future and your future because Jesus was in the loins of Ruth and Boaz.

In Ruth 3:1–4 we find Naomi giving great wisdom. In verse 5, Ruth responded: "All that you say to me I will do." Really, that one phrase is the only necessary phrase you need to know and embrace to receive confidence that you have a future! Tell fear of the future to leave you now, and be willing to do whatever you need to do to obey the voice of the Lord, and your future will be intact.

CHAPTER 3

IN THE **PROCESS** OF **TIME, GOD WILL VISIT!**
(DON'T GET LOST IN THE PROCESS)

P ROCESS IS A WONDERFUL WORD TO UNDERSTAND SINCE YOUR whole life is one! Process involves a progressive course or tendency to accomplish a desire. This desire can be within you, it can be someone else's desire for you, or it can originate from a divine source. The gradual progress of developing a course of action and proceeding with the operations necessary to accomplish an overall project is part of what we call process. Process can include experimentation. Process includes a series of changes that result in growth or decay. Process is linked with passage. This is what makes *process* a "time" word.

In law, "the whole course of proceedings, in a cause, real or personal, civil or criminal, from the original writ to the end of suit" is a process. "*Original process* is the means taken to compel the defendant to appear in court. *Mesne process* is that which issues, pending the suit, upon some collateral or interlocu-

> *Braving storms in the midst of our process is a key element to our faith.*

tory matter. *Final process* is the process of execution."[1] This will become more important to understand as we discuss how Satan changes laws and times, but, as you can see, most of our processes have a process.

PROCEED UNTIL YOU GET THERE

For a process to be complete you must *proceed*. This is what links process to our narrow transitions and making it through to the destination that God has for us. *Proceed* means to move, pass, or go forward from one place to another. I love how Jesus told His disciples, "We are going to the other side." (See one example in Mark 4:35.) He would either send them across without Him, or He would get in the boat and go with them. We have several accounts in the Bible where the winds, waves, and storm caught them halfway to their destination.

In Matthew 14, He goes out to meet them so He can help them get past their fear and reach the place where He has sent them. Braving storms in the midst of our process is a key element to our faith. Jesus said, "Why are you fearful, O you of little faith?" (Matt. 8:26). This did not mean that His disciples had *no faith*. Rather, it meant their faith was too little to get them to the next place He had for them. You must learn to proceed until you get to your "there."

Another good example of proceeding can be found in the life of Abraham. When Abraham was called out of Ur of the Chaldees, he and his family made it to Haran. His father, Terah, died in Haran. However, the Lord had a promised place for Abraham to get to. Haran was halfway between Ur of the Chaldees and Canaan, the Promised Land. If Abraham had ever stopped going or proceeding forth, we would not have seen the Lord make covenant with him to develop a people and give them a firstfruits land that all nations would revolve around. In Genesis 14:13, we find Abram being called "the Hebrew." The word *Hebrew* means one who crosses over. God made covenant with a man who would always proceed or cross over. All of us who are grafted into that covenant are people who are meant to proceed, cross over, or get to the other side.

Another great example is the Red Sea crossing in Exodus 14:1–2: "Now the LORD spoke to Moses, saying: 'Speak to the children of Israel, that they turn and camp before Pi Hahiroth, between Migdol and the sea.'" The children of Israel had proceeded from Egypt but were only halfway to their freedom. Pi Hahiroth was halfway between Egypt and the Red Sea crossing. At every halfway point, you must wait for your next instruction before you proceed. However, you must not settle for getting only halfway there.

As you proceed, the process you are in takes you from one state to another. As you read this book, you are in a process. If you are reading the chapters sequentially, you are proceeding in the process of under-standing and interpreting time better.

In John 8:42, Jesus said, "...for I proceeded forth and came from God." Jesus is both explaining His origination and predicting His departure. In other words, Jesus knew where He came from as well as the duration of time in which He would present the likeness of Father to us. Then He knew where He was going. Verse 58 says, "Before Abraham was, I AM." This was the same *I AM* who revealed Himself to Moses and led the children of Israel out of Egypt. This was the same *I AM* who revealed Jesus to Peter. *I AM* has always been in the process of manifesting. He was there before time and will be there after time.

When you advance, you make progress and get closer to completing the process you are in. From a legal standpoint, as you begin an action and the action becomes a series of actions and measures, you could get lost on how to proceed in your offense or defense. Most processes have a methodical, sequential manner of procession about them. In business and commerce you must make transactions in order to prosper. Your transactions must be interjected at the right place and the right time for ultimate prosperity to occur. Many times we believe we are prospering based upon the standards of the world. The danger of evaluating your progress in light of the world's definition of success is that the cultures of nations invade the ultimate process that God has for a people. Before long, you are conformed to the world as opposed to transforming society to reflect God's kingdom plan.

GO FORTH!

Go forth! Get up and advance! Just proceed forward with caution! In Hebrew, *proceed* is the word *yatsa'*, which means "to come forth, go out, go forth, bring out, come out." This verb is used more than a thousand times in the Bible. Basically, this word means "movement away" from some point as you approach another point. This usually represents the departing point of a journey. The first place that *yatsa'* is used in the Bible is in Genesis 2:10, where we find that a river "came forth" or "flowed out" from the Garden of Eden.

Our enemies usually come forth to challenge us at an appropriate time. In 1 Samuel 17:4, Goliath, the champion of the Philistines, "went out" from the camp and challenged the Israelites. This word connotes that there is a *constant activity* that surrounds your day until you finally get to the place of rest that has been destined for you to reach. In a military campaign, you are in a process, or proceeding, in war until you either win or lose a battle. You come and go and engage in wars until you have secured the borders and boundaries that you have been given to protect.

Think about this situation. Goliath would taunt the army of the enemy all day long. He actually did this for forty days straight.

The concept of coming out and going forth is linked to the birth process.

Then David, a young shepherd boy, was sent on the war scene. He heard the enemy's voice, and he said, "Enough is enough," and started a new process. The process David started was to reverse and overthrow the process of the Philistine giant. David stopped the process of defeat that was working against the army of Israel and started a very short process that by the end of the day resulted in victory.

The concept of coming out and going forth is linked to the birth process as well. We will look more thoroughly at the process of giving birth in the chapter on travail. When viewing time, this "going forth" principle is very important to understand. We can never understand the concept of harvest or moving from one harvest season to another if we do not embrace the time sequences involved in going forth.

One of my favorite chapters in the Bible is Exodus 23. God links the law with time and the need to gather and meet with Him three times a year. He shares that if we stay in time and walk justly, He will send an angel before us to help us proceed to the place He has destined and promised us. If we rebel against His messenger and the help He sends, then we will wander, and the processes He has planned for our development will be prolonged.

GOD CAN GO OUT!

When applied to God, the action of *going out* only infrequently refers to His *abandoning* a certain location. In Ezekiel 10:18, the glory of the Lord left or "departed from the threshold of the temple and stood over the cherubim." Eventually it departed from the temple altogether (v. 19).

Often this verb pictures the Lord as *going forth* to aid His people, especially in texts suggesting or depicting His appearances among men. In Egypt, the Lord *went out* into the midst of the Egyptians to smite their firstborn (Exod. 11:4–5). The Lord's departure point in such cases is sometimes represented as "Seir," as in Judges 5:4 where He left the region until Deborah arose to defend Israel.[2]

Because God goes out, we know that God is on the move—moving, leaving, or inhabiting space and time with us. One good example is the cloud by day and the fire by night. In Exodus 14:13–23 (TLB), we find the story of the people who needed to proceed but were stopped by a blockade:

> But Moses told the people, "Don't be afraid. Just stand where you are and watch, and you will see the wonderful way the Lord will rescue you today. The Egyptians you are looking at—you will never see them again. The Lord will fight for you, and you won't need to lift a finger!"
>
> Then the Lord said to Moses, "Quit praying and get the people moving! Forward, march! Use your rod—hold it out over the water, and the sea will open up a path before you, and all the people of Israel shall walk through on dry ground! I will harden the hearts of the Egyptians, and they will go in after you and you will see the honor I will get in defeating Pharaoh and all his armies, chariots, and horsemen. And all Egypt shall know that I am Jehovah."
>
> Then the Angel of God, who was leading the people of Israel, moved the cloud around behind them, and it stood between the

people of Israel and the Egyptians. And that night, as it changed to a pillar of fire, it gave darkness to the Egyptians but light to the people of Israel! So the Egyptians couldn't find the Israelis!

Meanwhile, Moses stretched his rod over the sea, and the Lord opened up a path through the sea, with walls of water on each side; and a strong east wind blew all that night, drying the sea bottom. So the people of Israel walked through the sea on dry ground! Then the Egyptians followed them between the walls of water along the bottom of the sea—all of Pharaoh's horses, chariots, and horsemen.

As we obey Him in one generation, we create a legacy for the next generation.

The Lord was saying, "Moses, don't fear; you have prayed enough. I have a plan. Get ready to proceed. Use your authority, and I will use My power. We will win this thing we are in! You get the people moving, and I will move behind you and deal with your enemies!" In my life, I have found that when I move into place and proceed forward, exercising the authority that I have been given, the Lord moves into place, positions Himself, and helps me overcome all the enemies that are surrounding me.

CRITICALLY REVIEW YOUR LIFE

Our Red Seas can be difficult times. We must discern the situation. We must always take a critical look at what we are doing. We find ourselves always asking: *Why? When? How? Who? Where?* This is part of development, but it must not be the only element that interacts in our process. We must be a people who think faith! Whatever He says to do, we just obey. The problem comes in waiting and watching. The time element of our obedience seems to be the catalyst that changes the course of our life.

Kaizen, or continuous improvement, is the hallmark of the Toyota Production System. The primary objectives are to identify and eliminate all waste. Kaizen also strives to ensure quality. Its key elements emphasize making a task simpler and easier to perform, re-engineering processes, increasing the speed and efficiency of the work process, and constantly improving quality.

...By asking why and by trying to eliminate unnecessary steps and duplication, we can save time and dollars that can then be used for more productive purposes. By focusing on quality, working with hiring managers to define it, and then tracking it, you can significantly improve how you are perceived within your organization.

Vast improvements can be made incrementally and without great cost. There is often much more to be gained by working to improve what we have before investing heavily in new technologies that we are not sure how to use well and that may not even meet our current needs....

Toyota...[has] adopted an overall philosophy of evolutionary change. They make small changes, all the time, under the concept known as *continuous improvement.* For Toyota there is never a *completed* stage, but just an ongoing series of tweaks.[3]

This philosophy of continuous improvement works very well in the field of manufacturing and production. Perhaps God is even *tweaking us* from generation to generation until we become spotless and without wrinkle. As we obey Him in one generation, we create a legacy for the next generation. However, our decisions are not always as cut and dried as developing a product like an automobile. In the spiritual realm, our process is affected by subjective issues. Your desires, emotions, expectations, past experiences, misperceived communications, fears, and misinterpreted nuances all play a part in your tweaking and your entrance into the future. These subjective criteria create developments that highly effect your process to get to your *there.* Consequently, do not overprocess your life and what is happening around you, lest you miss the opportunity in time to experience change.

Time Has a Process

In *God's Timing for Your Life*, Dutch Sheets says:

> At the Pool of Bethesda, Jesus came to the man who had been in his paralyzed condition for 36 years and asked him what seemed to be a strange question: "Do you want to get well?" (John 5:6, NIV). The man's answer revealed that although he was waiting at the pool, he really had no hope of being healed. He was in a *kairos* moment, close to fullness, but hopelessness had set in. Jesus asked him this question to make him realize that, although he was waiting for the miraculous stirring in the pool, he had lost all hope of actually being healed. Only seconds away from experiencing the new, just a handclasp away from total restoration, the man was too disillusioned to recognize it. Somewhere along the way, as he went through the process of time, he lost his expectation. There wasn't anything within him that could respond in hope to Jesus' question. When God brings a shift, we must be ready to shift with Him. If we're not careful, we won't believe that He can bring us from the *chronos* stages through the *kairos* seasons and into fullness.[4]

Actually, the man at the pool of Bethesda could not just answer the Lord's question. He overprocessed the situation. The Lord wanted a simple yes or no—"Yes, I want to be healed," or "No, I do not want to be healed." Instead, the man gave the Lord the reasons *why* he had not been healed and how he perceived the situation he was in. Thank God the Lord bypassed all of that and healed him anyway.

The words and promises we read in the Bible do not just float through the air and never interact with time and space. The Author, God, and those who penned for Him relate time to teaching content, faith, and action. The Bible is a record of happenings in history that pervade time to reach into the present and extend into the future. When God and man meet, the principles in the Word of God manifest and become a reality in time. These *events* are tangible and allow us to measure and weigh a faith action or supernatural interaction and determine that heaven's plan has invaded Earth's atmosphere.

GOD, JESUS, AND HISTORY

God spoke through events in history. He spoke to Noah and saved mankind by giving a plan for an ark. (This was a major shift in the earth since there were no boats and no rain.) He made covenant with Abraham. He redeemed Israel from slavery. He revealed the Torah to man. He filled the temple of Solomon with His glory. He sent His Son into the world to buy back mankind from the clutches of the enemy. He knit together each of us in our mother's womb and then placed us in time. When we are born, a new history begins.

When God meets and communes with man, and man obeys God, history changes. God and man relating to each other in time creates an event in history. When the Spirit manifests itself through God's presence, a history of God in time is developed. As we accept the divine intervention of God with Abraham, and then accept the sacrifice of His Son, Jesus, we are grafted into the eternal covenant of God, which pervades time. We work with the overall plan of a Divine Engineer to bring about the fullness of the earth.

One question we usually ask or at least think is, "What really did happen in the past?" I love the old song "I Love to Tell the Story." As a kid, family gatherings always included singing. Our family would sit around, someone would play the piano, and we would sing. Then we usually ended up under a big chinaberry tree listening to stories. I was a very inquisitive child, so I asked a lot of questions and heard a lot of stories. The events of each story were always interpreted by whoever was telling the story. Therefore, some stories sounded different based upon the storyteller.

You remember your past through the stories—truth or myth—that you have heard from others or have told yourself.

63

You remember your past through the stories—truth or myth—that you have heard from others or have told yourself. A *myth* is filled with symbols and summarizes the past with different types of interpretations. In many cases, the event would take on new meaning based upon the myth of the story instead of the actual facts of the story.

This is how I have approached my Bible readings. I sit with the Spirit of God to hear the story of the Word. I am very interested in the history and events that occurred, which are written about in the Bible. With this perspective of wanting to hear from the Author of the story Himself, I have asked the question, "Who is Jesus?" I have always wanted to know about the events taking place in His life that led Him from birth to crucifixion. Because of the *myth of the event*, the uniqueness of history is something that is hard to comprehend. Many times we want the ease of placing history into a cycle that is related to a process that will repeat itself. However, there are unique categories, moments, and events that are necessary for the understanding of history, since that which is individual cannot be comprehended in terms of generalities. General cycles in history give us the key to the knowledge of space. The uniqueness of an event is the key to the understanding of time.

The life of Jesus was an event that changed the course of history. The life of Jesus from birth to crucifixion changed the course of time for humanity. The resurrection of Jesus changed the course of time through eternity. This unique event, God coming to the earth in human form, redeemed man and created a way for restoration of the past and development of the future. This event removed the cycle of decay and hopelessness and gave us the authority to rule in a world of confusion.

YOUR LIFE—AN EVENT IN TIME

Psalm 139 explains your life as an event. Most of us never recognize our lives as events in which God has participated from the beginning. Therefore, many people do not see themselves as history makers or changers! Stop for a moment and read Psalm 139, and allow the Spirit of God to take you back from where you are today to the event of your beginning!

O Lord, You have searched me and known me.
You know my sitting down and my rising up;
You understand my thought afar off.
You comprehend my path and my lying down,
And are acquainted with all my ways.
For there is not a word on my tongue,
But behold, O Lord, You know it altogether.
You have hedged me behind and before,
And laid Your hand upon me.
Such knowledge is too wonderful for me;
It is high, I cannot attain it.

Where can I go from Your Spirit?
Or where can I flee from Your presence?
If I ascend into heaven, You are there;
If I make my bed in hell, behold, You are there.
If I take the wings of the morning,
And dwell in the uttermost parts of the sea,
Even there Your hand shall lead me,
And Your right hand shall hold me.
If I say, "Surely the darkness shall fall on me,"
Even the night shall be light about me;
Indeed, the darkness shall not hide from You,
But the night shines as the day;
The darkness and the light are both alike to You.

For You formed my inward parts;
You covered me in my mother's womb.
I will praise You, for I am fearfully and wonderfully made;
Marvelous are Your works,
And that my soul knows very well.
My frame was not hidden from You,
When I was made in secret,
And skillfully wrought in the lowest parts of the earth.
Your eyes saw my substance, being yet unformed.
And in Your book they all were written,

The days fashioned for me,
When as yet there were none of them.

—Psalm 139:1–16

What an event! God was there, knitting you at the beginning and building within you the ability to change history and represent Him in the earth when we enter space and time. Not only is our life an event, but also once we are knit together, we find that God has a cycle of life for each of us. In *God's Now Time for Your Life*, Rebecca Wagner Sytsema and I write:

> This life cycle begins at conception and moves along in the following progression:
>
> 1. *Conception*: God begins His purpose for us by knitting us together in the womb.
> 2. *Birth*: The new life that God has created is brought forth.
> 3. *Age of accountability*: We gain an awareness of our need for God.
> 4. *Rebirth*: We are quickened from darkness into light. We must be born again.
> 5. *Receiving hope*: We search for and receive the expectation of God for our future.
> 6. *Maturing of our faith*: Our faith is matured into an overcoming weapon of God.
> 7. *Demonstration*: God demonstrates His power and wisdom, which unlocks our destiny.
> 8. *Manifestation*: God manifests His glory and inner fulfillment of our identity in Him.
> 9. *Completion*: Our role in the earthly realm is completed as we face death and enter into eternity.

The enemy loves to interrupt the life cycle in any one of these stages so that the fulfillment of our destiny cannot be completed.

He would love for us to miss the *kairos* or opportune time that the Lord has in each of these phases above. However, if you miss that now time, it doesn't mean that things will never be back in order. It just means that you will postpone what God wants to do and enter into a prolonged wilderness season.[5]

I want to encourage you to see yourself as God saw you when He was knitting you together with a destined purpose to perform. Your life may have taken many twists and turns, but the purpose is still there. Don't live in the past. Rather, allow the Spirit of the Lord to meet you today and reorder your steps so you proceed toward the *there* He has for you!

CHAPTER 4

THERE WILL COME A DAY

FROM GRECO-ROMAN THINKING, THE WORLD OF *SPACE* OR *COSMOS* was defined. However, the Lord communicated His concept of *time* to the Hebrew people. The Bible is a historical account of life. The greatest events ever recorded are there for any reader to experience. The Word of God not only gives us a historical analysis of God's interaction with man, but it also shows us how to live in the present, and it connects us to eternity. History witnesses God. God called the chaos of the world into an order. We then have an account of man's interaction with God's order.

We can view history as a series of events that reflect chaos, disorder, and bloodshed, or we can see history as God's record of man becoming who we were destined to be from the beginning. All the parts in history are like a puzzle. Each piece is fitting together to form the full plan of what God's will on the earth should be. God has been there from the beginning. He is involved in our coming, going, doings, and being.

I always tell my children that they are filled with potential. However, they must learn to make every day count and not miss their opportunities. God and man both have much at stake when we discuss time. God already knows how man must choose, but man must choose. If man does not choose each day to follow and serve God, man's greatest potential in time will not be fulfilled.

THERE IS A PERFECT MOMENT TO CRY OUT FOR GOD TO INTERVENE IN TIME

I love the story of how the people of God ended up in Egypt. In Genesis 15:13–16, when God made His covenant with Abraham, He prophesied to him:

> Know certainly that your descendants will be strangers in a land that is not theirs, and will serve them, and they will afflict them four hundred years. And also the nation whom they serve I will judge; afterward they shall come out with great possessions. Now as for you, you shall go to your fathers in peace; you shall be buried at a good old age. But in the fourth generation they shall return here, for the iniquity of the Amorites is not yet complete.

In a dream, God told Abraham what the future of this covenant would bring. Four generations or four hundred years would elapse with the people being afflicted. Then God would bring the people out from under their captivity and move them into their promised boundaries. Also during those four hundred years, He would be working on the land and the people within the boundaries He was promising to Abraham's people. Most of you know this story. Abraham's descendant Jacob had a son named Joseph, who was sold into slavery in Egypt. God then brought a famine upon the land where Jacob and his sons dwelt, and this caused the whole family to end up in Egypt with Joseph. I'll explain that in a later chapter. The Israelites settled in the land of Goshen in Egypt. They were favored there, and they actually prospered there more than the Egyptians, but this was only for a time; after several hundred years, things began to change.

Now let's move forward four hundred years. By this time, the Israelites were slaves to the Egyptians and were being used to build some of the structures of that nation.

In Exodus 2:23–25 we read the following:

Now it happened *in the process of time* that the king of Egypt died. Then the children of Israel groaned because of the bondage, and they cried out; and their cry came up to God because of the bondage. So God heard their groaning, and God remembered His covenant with Abraham, with Isaac, and with Jacob. And God looked upon the children of Israel, and God acknowledged them.

—EMPHASIS ADDED

There is a leadership change in Egypt. The favor the people have had in the past is removed, which causes a season of hard labor to begin for the Israelites. They had been accustomed to making bricks for the buildings of the Egyptians, but the Egyptians later removed the straw that was used in their brick

> *The Lord, who is not in time, waits to hear a sound coming out of time.*

making, making their labor a difficult, hard situation. God was in this situation! It was His perfect timing to produce a change so that the covenant He had with this people would come into fullness.

Are you aware that many of your situations are like this? God is using those hard things in your life that you go through to produce the fullness of His promise in you. Notice what happens here—the people CRY OUT! *The Lord, who is not in time, waits to hear a sound coming out of time.* He then steps into time, remembers His covenant with us, and then begins to visit and give us our plan of deliverance. In this case, He came down and caused a bush to burn.

Exodus 3:2–4 says:

And the Angel of the LORD appeared to him in a flame of fire from the midst of a bush. So he looked, and behold, the bush was burning with fire, but the bush was not consumed. Then Moses said, "I will now turn aside and see this great sight, why the bush does not burn." So when the LORD saw that he turned aside to look, God called to him from the midst of the bush and said, "Moses, Moses!" And he said, "Here I am."

I love what is recorded here. Moses "turned aside" to see why the bush on fire did not burn. At that moment God revealed Himself to him as I AM, the absolute *I*, the self-existent *One*. In the midst of your circumstances, are you watching for God to come down? Are you willing to turn aside from your daily activities to see and commune with Him?

The Suddenlies Are Very Difficult to Understand

I call this experience with Moses a "suddenly." There comes a time when God, man, and time are all aligned! That produces a suddenly. *Suddenly* means that in an unexpected manner, something will happen without us being notified. This can be a result of some violent or passionate occurrence. Whatever creates the suddenly, it is an unexpected surprise that comes into our path. If we are not already prepared for this happening, we don't have time to get prepared.

Suddenlies are hard to understand because of the surprise element. The surprise element creates an emotional response in us. Many times in our *waiting for God to move* we get weary of looking for a suddenly. When we least expect Him to move, He moves, and we miss it.

One of the most balanced biblical accounts of a suddenly is the story of the passing of the mantle from Elijah to Elisha. In 1 Kings 19, Elijah is instructed by the Lord to give his mantle to Elisha. He finds Elisha in the field and throws the mantle upon him. I have heard so many interpret this story as being the time in which Elisha "received" the mantle. From a prophetic standpoint, this has merit. However, you find that the experience became the beginning point, the moment in time when Elisha left behind his family and vocation and began to follow Elijah.

All believers have experienced this. God often reveals to us His intentions for our lives, whether personally or prophetically through someone else, far in advance of when He intends for them to occur. When they don't immediately come to pass, many of us become confused. Abraham, who was promised Isaac twenty-five years in advance, certainly did. So did David, who was anointed to be king over Israel twenty years before it transpired. The frustration and confusion set in because this timeless God doesn't always bother to tell us that what He is promising may be years ahead of fulfillment, just as He did with Abraham and David.

With the decree of the Lord, we row backward into our destiny.

In 2 Kings 2:11, seven years after Elijah first met Elisha, we read: "Then it happened, as they continued on and talked, that suddenly a chariot of fire appeared with horses of fire, and separated the two of them; and Elijah went up by a whirlwind into heaven." Elisha asked for a double portion of the spirit of Elijah. Elijah told him that this would be a very hard thing, but if he followed him to the end, then he could receive that double portion. Every ensuing relationship attempted to turn Elisha from this path. Elijah would even encourage him to turn around and go in a different direction. However, when Elisha followed Elijah to the end, Elisha was present when a chariot took Elijah into heaven.

What you see in the natural must be processed in the spiritual.

Notice, this was a suddenly! After seven years, the suddenly occurred, and Elisha received both the mantle of Elijah and a double portion of his spirit. Do not grow weary in waiting and following after what God has promised you. God, you, and the supernatural culmination of events and faith acts can all come together in one moment. Perhaps there is a suddenly waiting for you at any moment.

WE MUST KEEP GOING

The key to Elisha experiencing this suddenly was that he kept following. Many of us never get to our destination because we quit going. There are many elements and circumstances that influence your times and seasons in the earth. Adverse circumstances may come into your life, blockades may arise on your path, or your vision may get blocked. You must never forget that what you see in the natural must be processed in the spiritual. You must continue to grow and mature spiritually. You must keep going!

Jesus called all of His disciples and those He was teaching to follow Him. In the process of time, if you will keep your face set like a flint, just as Jesus demonstrated to us when He walked the earth realm, you will reach your destination. It was over a period of three years that Jesus taught His followers what they needed to know so that history would be affected and God's kingdom would be advanced.

God stepped out of time and came to the earth to save us. Jesus was the perfect image of God the Father, and He taught us how to walk "in time." Here are some time-sensitive events to which we can all relate.

1. We must go beyond our current levels of celebration and religious ritual.

In John 2, Jesus and His mother were invited to a wedding. His disciples attended with Him. Weddings in Jewish culture were events of celebration. The celebrations were meant to last seven days. Prophetically, a wedding represented the Feast of Tabernacles, which I will talk about in the next chapter. During the wedding ceremony the vows would be exchanged midweek, and then they would celebrate until the Sabbath. In the wedding at Cana, the celebration was coming to a close too early. The wedding party had run out of wine, which was a disgrace. Mary said to Jesus, "'They have no wine.' Jesus said to her, 'Woman, what does your concern have to do with Me? My hour has not yet come'" (John 2:3–4). Timing is so important when beginning a new thrust or season of life. Mary continued by encouraging the servants to do whatever Jesus told them to do. Jesus then asked them to bring water pots that were normally used for religious purification ceremonies. Once those pots were filled to the brim with water, He turned the water into wine.

Then the wedding host exclaimed, "Every man at the beginning sets out the good wine, and when the guests have well drunk, then the inferior. You have kept the good wine until now!" (v. 10). The wedding party had advanced to the next level of celebration. What had been used for religious ritual now was used for festive celebration. This was a picture of what was to come. Jesus said He did this because this act was the *beginning* of the revelation of His glory, so that His disciples would believe.

At first, this does not appear to be the beginning of the next phases of Jesus's life and teaching. Jesus could do nothing but what the Father told Him to do. Evidently, the Father told Him, "Begin now to reveal Your glory." Once He started revealing His glory, He knew He would have to go all the way until that revelation became complete in the fullness of time.

2. We must go beyond our poverty way of thinking and enter into a harvest-multiplication thought mode.

First Kings 17 is the story of the prophet Elijah coming on the scene to deal with the spiritual atmosphere of idolatry that had overtaken Israel. He began by making a spiritual decree and legislating the heavens. He declared the heavens would produce no dew or rain except at his word. This decree affected him along with everyone else. He left where he was and went to the brook called Cherith, which eventually dried up because of no rain.

To find a supply of water, he had to keep moving. The Lord told him to go to Zarephath, where he would find a widow at the gates of the city. The drought that he had proclaimed had affected the entire region. When he arrived at Zarephath, he saw a widow who was picking up sticks and preparing for her last meal. This was the woman who God said would take care of him. However, this woman was filled with a poverty mentality and with despair. He instructed her to go home, take whatever she had left in her cupboard, and prepare him a meal *first*. By faith, she did this. Her obedience created enough supply for them to be sustained over the next three years. Once she broke through her poverty and gave her *firstfruits* to the prophet, supply did not run out.

3. We must also go beyond our debt mentality and know that the Lord can free us to accomplish His purposes.

In 2 Kings 4, Elisha had his own experience with a widow. This widow was in terrible debt. The debtors were coming to take her entire inheritance, including her children. She went to the prophet and explained her situation to him. In verse 2, Elisha says, "'What shall I do for you? Tell me, what do you have in the house?' And she said, 'Your maidservant has nothing in the house but a jar of oil.'" If we understand the *law of use* we can get past our debt structure. The prophet told her to go to all of her neighbors, borrow all their vessels, and then pour all her available oil until all of the vessels were filled. Upon selling the oil, she would have enough to overcome her debt. Do not allow debt structures to put you into debt. God will give you a strategy to break the debt structure that has come to control your times and future.

4. We must come to the end of ourselves and know that God has a better plan.

In Luke 5, Jesus chose to move away from the pressing crowd, and He borrowed a boat from His fisherman disciples. After He finished teaching the crowd, He told Peter, one of the disciples, to launch out into the deep for a great catch. Peter explained to Him that he and the other fishermen had been out in that area fishing all night long and had caught nothing. However, out of *respect*, not faith, Peter did what the Lord asked him to do. When they reached the "deep portion" of the sea, Jesus told him to cast the net opposite of what he did the night before. Peter pulled in such a catch that he had to call for his business partners and use their boat also. This brought Peter to a place of repentance. Because of the Lord's strategy, which produced an overabundance of supply, Peter was overwhelmed. He admitted that he was an unworthy man. Jesus used that instance to explain to Peter that it wasn't really about the fish but about *the future* and what He would do in days ahead.

Do not allow what you have done in the past that has not produced to keep you from doing something today that will produce. Do not allow yesterday to defeat you today. The Lord has a plan today that can open up your entire future.

5. We must go beyond our past failures and structures of unbelief that would hold us captive and prevent us from accomplishing our future.

In Acts 12 you find a young church finding its way in the midst of persecution. Herod had cut off the apostle James's head and now had

Peter imprisoned. Verse 5 says, "Peter was therefore kept in prison, but constant prayer was offered to God for him by the church." This time the church began to pray. They could not allow the death of James to keep them from praying in a new way. They prayed. God sent an angel who led Peter out of prison. When Peter showed up at the house of Mary, the mother of John, Rhoda the doorkeeper heard Peter's knock, opened the door, and could not fathom that God had really answered their prayers. Everyone in the prayer meeting was in a measure of unbelief over the Lord breaking through in this situation. Keep going past all of your unbelief, your last measure of faith and prayer, and any defeat that has tried to stop you in the past so that you can unlock your future today.

6. We must be aware of every opportunity that the Lord has set before us and not miss the open windows and doors of heaven that come into our spheres of influence.

In 2 Kings 13, we read the story of King Joash, who was in a terrible trial with the nation of Syria. He visited Elisha, who was on his deathbed. The prophet told him to perform a prophetic act by shooting an arrow through the window toward Syria in the east. Then Elisha instructed him to take arrows and strike the ground, representing the defeat of the Syrians. Joash struck the ground three times. Elisha rose from his deathbed in anger and rebuked this half-hearted demonstration of faith. Joash missed his opportunity to destroy Syria. In the same way, you can easily miss your window of opportunity by not being passionate and taking full advantage of the time in which God has set you to accomplish the victories ahead in your life.

7. The Lord knows the beginning from the end.

He is Alpha and Omega. If you cooperate with Him, you will experience the best in your generation. Many times the Lord will tell you what He longs to do. He will show you the whole picture. That is how vision works. Sometimes what you see in the beginning becomes misty the further along you go. If that happens, the strong faith you had in the beginning can become but a dream. However, you must remember that when God shows you something in the beginning, often He is revealing the end to you, and if you just keep going, you will step into the fullness of His plan, which is waiting for you on your road ahead.

Rowing Into the Future

As Dutch Sheets and I traveled the United States together, I would hear him teaching on *alignment.* Two of his favorite verses are:

> Declaring the end from the beginning,
> And from ancient times things which have not been done,
> Saying, "My purpose will be established,
> And I will accomplish all My good pleasure."
> —Isaiah 46:10, nasu

The other is from a prophecy that God gave Jeremiah as he warned the people of their captivity ahead.

> "For I know the plans that I have for you," declares the Lord, "plans for welfare and not for calamity to give you a future and a hope."
> —Jeremiah 29:11, nasu

These are both time-sensitive scriptures. The words translated "end" and "future" are the same Hebrew word, *achariyth,* and when fully understood bring powerful insight. The New King James Version translates this word as "destiny." Spiros Zodhiates says the following about it:

> The general meaning is "after," "later," "behind," "following." The Hebrew way of thinking was like a man rowing a boat; he backs into the future. Therefore, what is "behind" and what is "future" come from the same root *achar.*[1]

You can read the account of our travels to all fifty states in *Releasing the Prophetic Destiny of a Nation.* In that book, Dutch says the following concerning this concept of time:

Fascinating—what is behind and what is future comes from the same word. Actually, within its meaning is captured the concept of eternity—in both directions, past and future—depicting the eternal nature of God and the spirit realm.

It is very encouraging that our destiny and future are in the hands of an eternal God who declares "the end from the beginning!" And while it does seem that we row backward into our future—by faith, without fully seeing in advance what is coming—we nevertheless know that our destiny is secure in God, and that our end can always be greater than our beginning.

As I meditated on this verse, Isaiah 46:10, especially the part about God decreeing the end (*achariyth*) from the beginning, the Holy Spirit impressed upon me an interesting phrase: *Eventually time catches up with My decree.* In other words, the eternal, timeless God declares the end from the beginning; and as I continue to row into my future, I will eventually row into that which He has destined and decreed for me.[2]

THE POWER OF SAYING WHAT GOD IS SAYING

I love what the Bible teaches us about decrees and the words of our mouth. Job 22:27–30 (AMP) says:

You will make your prayer to Him, and He will hear you, and you will pay your vows. You shall also decide and decree a thing, and it shall be established for you; and the light [of God's favor] shall shine upon your ways. When they make [you] low, you will say, [There is] a lifting up; and the humble person He lifts up and saves. He will even deliver the one [for whom you intercede] who is not innocent; yes, he will be delivered through the cleanness of your hands.

Also, in Job 28 we find the power of the Lord's words:

> Then He saw wisdom and declared it; He prepared it, indeed, He searched it out.
>
> —JOB 28:27, NKJV

A *decree* is an official order, edict, or decision. A decree is something that seems to be foreordained. This is what makes decrees prophetic. To *decree* can also mean to order, decide, or officially appoint a group or person to accomplish something. A decree is linked with setting apart or ordaining something or someone. A *declaration* is an announcement, a formal statement, or a proclamation. This statement sometimes is what a plaintiff releases in his complaint, which results in a court action. A proclamation actually brings something into a more official realm. A proclamation can ban, outlaw, or restrict. This is linked with the process of binding and loosing.

Once we hear the word of the Lord decreed, declared, or proclaimed, God begins to establish this word in the earth realm. This causes God's people to press in for a full manifestation of what He is longing to accomplish in our midst. All through the Word of God you find decrees, declarations, and proclamations. Cyrus sent out a decree that caused God's people to return from captivity and rebuild the city of Jerusalem and the temple of God. Caesar sent out a decree that positioned Mary and Joseph in the place where prophecy could be fulfilled through the birth of Jesus. Elijah declared that the heavens would be shut up. The priests proclaimed what God was ordaining.

As Dutch and I traveled to each state, we knew that this was our mandate. We were assured by the Spirit that God had a unique *word* for each state.

Another verse that Dutch used often was Job 22:28 (NASU):

> You will also decree a thing, and it will be established for you; and light will shine on your ways.

The word *thing* in this verse is *omer*, and it means a word, promise, or decree.[3]

Dutch shares:

> This portion of the verse could be translated, "You will decree a decree." When time catches up to the decree of the Lord for our lives—when the opportune time for fulfillment has come—we must decree the decree, agreeing with and declaring what God has said about us. As we come into agreement with His plans by declaring our faith in them, we are releasing the creative power of His word, which, as the verse goes on to say, will cause them to be established.[4]

You must learn to hear His plans, discern His timing, and decree the decrees that will bring change to your life and what you are responsible for in your sphere of authority. One of the most important questions you should ask is this: What are You saying to me right now? Once you discern or hear what the Lord is saying, you can come into agreement with His plans and purposes. There is tremendous power in being in harmony with God and His will in heaven. When we think that He declared this will from the beginning of time, and then we release the creative power of His word into our NOW season, the beginning and the end come together in time and a manifestation of His glory occurs.

As stated earlier, Abraham the Hebrew was the one who crossed over. We are a people who must keep crossing over. We must find our prototypes or models for this generation. We must identify the apostolic leaders who are developing those prototypes. In *Releasing the Prophetic Destiny of a Nation*, I wrote the following:

> The four walls of the Church must expand to encompass all societal structures. We must identify apostolic kingdom prototypes where Church leaders and economic leaders are working together to bring transformation to their community. We must identify the apostolic leaders who are willing to shift their minds from maintenance/ pasturing to dominion. We must carefully watch signs in the earth

and identify new fields and people groups where the time is ripe for Kingdom invasion.[5]

Can the Lord birth a nation in a day? The answer is a simple yes! If we keep watching and responding by faith to a holy God, we will eventually see Him in our midst moving and changing situations around us that reflect His will in heaven.

This pattern and redemptive process is very relevant to all of us. God wants to reveal His purposes and expose the tactics of the enemy to abort them. He wants to give His strategy for recovery and fulfillment. His desire is that your *latter* always be greater than your *former*. Even when loss has occurred in your life, He has a plan to restore you beyond the place you departed. Haggai, a restorative prophet, gave this prophecy in a season when God had brought His people out of Babylonian captivity to rebuild Jerusalem and restore the temple, yet the Lord's directives were not being fulfilled. The people returned and restoration began, but they got discouraged in their process of rebuilding.

Even when loss has occurred in your life, He has a plan to restore you beyond the place you departed.

The warfare around them caused them to grow disinterested and disillusioned in their mission. Because of opposition, the work on the temple was stopped for sixteen years. Haggai, along with Zechariah, began to bring a word of correction and challenge to get the people going again and complete what they had begun. God's plan for blessing and provision to be like an overflowing river had caused it to become a trickling stream because they had abandoned God's project for their own. At the rebuke of the prophet, God's children responded by repenting and renewing their efforts, thereby ending this sixteen-year delay. Many times we delay the will of God in the earth realm because we fail to endure the warfare that encompasses our God assignments.

It is about this very thing that Haggai prophesied in Haggai 2:9 (NASU):

"The latter glory of this house will be greater than the former," says the LORD of hosts, "and in this place I will give peace," declares the LORD of hosts.

This is a timeless promise that all of us have access to embrace. His plan and desire are always that we go from glory to glory (2 Cor. 3:18), faith to faith (Rom. 1:17), and for the latter to be greater than the former. In the midst of our trials, testings, and even losses, we must ask ourselves the question, Will we rise up and complete what we have begun and what He is waiting to see come to an end?

THERE IS A TIME

There is a time to start and a time to complete. God is Alpha and Omega. He has a beginning and an end in everything He does. Ecclesiastes 3 says:

To everything there is a season,
A time for every purpose under heaven:
A time to be born,
   And a time to die;
A time to plant,
   And a time to pluck what is planted;
A time to kill,
   And a time to heal;
A time to break down,
   And a time to build up;
A time to weep,
   And a time to laugh;
A time to mourn,
   And a time to dance;
A time to cast away stones,
   And a time to gather stones;
A time to embrace,
   And a time to refrain from embracing;
A time to gain,
   And a time to lose;

A time to keep,
    And a time to throw away;
A time to tear,
    And a time to sew;
A time to keep silence,
    And a time to speak;
A time to love,
    And a time to hate;
A time of war,
    And a time of peace.

—ECCLESIASTES 3:1–8

Since we are "under heaven" we must be aware of time! I have served as a project manager several times in my secular vocations, but I still am a project manager. Intercession is like a project! God has chosen us as the necessary link to bring His will from heaven to the earth. He wants us to commune with Him, listen carefully to His voice, gain prophetic revelation, and decree that revelation into the earth. This will unlock miracles, overthrow iniquities and strongholds, and release His blessings.

EMBRACING TIME BY UNDERSTANDING

The easiest way for us to understand time is to think of an action or condition that exists or continues and is measured by its period of duration. Time can be measured in hours, days, weeks, months, years, seasons, or dispensations. The above passage in Ecclesiastes 3 is a key in understanding *present time*. There is a time for every purpose, and time has a duration attached to that purpose. We do not know our time, but our times are in the hands of the Lord who knit us together in our mother's womb. If we trust in Him, we will be able to see Him in the midst of our time (Ps. 31:15). We should never believe that we possess our own times.

Now is a time to expect the next move of the Holy Spirit to begin!

Only when we are doing the will of the Lord is time multiplying on our behalf (James 4:13–17).

There is an *acceptable NOW time* when God manifests Himself to all mankind. He would have all of mankind be saved. There is a day of salvation for each one of us (2 Cor. 6:2). We are not to fret over evildoers. Even though evil is multiplying in the world, we must remember that we can redeem time (Eph. 5:16). We must learn to see God working in the present time-and-space world within which we live. If we do this, our present time will be used for God's glory.

God promised Abraham and Sarah that they would have a child in their lifetime. The reality of this promise seemed to fade from manifestation the older the two of them became. However, there was a day when the promise was fulfilled. I call this the *fulfillment of time*. If we are daily walking, expecting, and watching for God to manifest His glory, eventually we will step into times of fulfillment. I also believe that God has seasons for fulfillment. I love how Peter refers to the prophecy in Joel 2 in his sermon recorded in Acts 2 when the people are appearing drunk and are speaking in tongues. What he actually does is say, "This is that..." (Acts 2:16, KJV). That's how fulfillment works. God warned Jeremiah that Jerusalem would fall and the people would go into captivity. He was also able to say, "This is that!"

Many times we do not have the opportunity of seeing the manifestation of what has been prophesied. Daniel prophesied much about world empires and the judgment of nations. He never actually *saw* what he prophesied. This is how you understand *future time*. There are certain situations that have been set in time for a season or generations that have yet to be created.

THERE COMES A DAY FOR CHANGE

There are seasons when all of the elements and events that have been spoken align, and in the midst of those alignments change occurs. Think of the oppression that was in the earth realm before Jesus came. There had been four hundred dark years. There is a recurring cycle of four hundred years that is linked with darkness. Another way to look at the four-hundred-year cycle is linked with freedom.

I love the Christmas song "O Come, O Come, Emmanuel":

> O come, O come, Emmanuel,
> And ransom captive Israel,
> That mourns in lonely exile here
> Until the Son of God appear.
>
> Rejoice! Rejoice!
> Emmanuel shall come to thee, O Israel.
>
> O come, Thou Rod of Jesse, free
> Thine own from Satan's tyranny;
> From depths of hell Thy people save,
> And give them victory over the grave.
>
> O come, Thou Root of Jesse's tree,
> An ensign of Thy people be;
> Before Thee rulers silent fall;
> All peoples on Thy mercy call.
>
> O come, Desire of nations, bind
> In one the hearts of all mankind;
> Bid Thou our sad divisions cease,
> And be Thyself our King of Peace.[6]

Even though this song was not available during the season before Jesus was born, it still gives us a great understanding of the heart cry of the people. O come, Emmanuel; we need You! We need You, King of Peace, to set us free.

Matthew 1:17 is an interesting scripture. We find: "So all the generations from Abraham to David are fourteen generations, from David until the captivity in Babylon are fourteen generations, and from the captivity in Babylon until the Christ are fourteen generations." Notice the three cycles of fourteen. When those three cycles of fourteen aligned,

Jesus came. There is a perfect time for heaven to enter into the earthly realm. The number fourteen means "passover, double, re-create, reproduce, disciple, servant, bond slave, employee; deliverance or salvation."[7] The number three denotes divine perfection. The time became perfect for Emmanuel to come and redeem mankind.

COMMUNICATION FROM HEAVEN PRODUCES REACTIONS IN THE EARTH

Notice how heaven began to communicate during this time frame. The stars aligned. Micah 5:2 (NIV) says, "But you, Bethlehem Ephrathah, though you are small among the clans of Judah, out of you will come for me one who will be ruler over Israel, whose origins are from of old, from ancient times." Numbers 24:17 and Isaiah 60:3 prophesy that a star would arise and light would come. As the universe communicated to the earth realm, the wise men of the East began to follow the star. For Mary, the angel Gabriel communicated and the Holy Spirit hovered or brooded over her. Angels came to visit the shepherds in the field who were watching their flock. Their normal day's work turned into a magnificent moment of change. The historical event that happened affected their day at work. The Spirit of God communicated to John the Baptist who would be the forerunner of the ministry of redemption while Jesus was in the womb.

Simeon and Anna had been crying out day and night for change to come to the earth. (See Luke 2:33–38.) If the above song had been written, they would have been singing it. They expected change. Therefore, when Jesus was presented to them, they immediately knew that He was the fulfillment of their prayers.

Are you expecting an alignment of events so He comes to visit your life today?

Prepare for Your Day of Visitation

We celebrate the Feast of Tabernacles each year. This has been a part of my family and church life for many years now. One year during the celebration the Lord said:

> Plant your feet! Ready yourself for change! You are entering a year of shaking and quaking! *This year will be known as the Year of Holy Spirit!* This will be the year the RIVERS will rise! Watch where heavens open and floods [physical] reach the earth, and document those places! Those are places targeted for a Holy Spirit invasion. Rising flood waters will cause you to move to higher ground. As the River of Holy Spirit rises, you will find yourself moving to the high places. I will position My people on the high places this year. As you worship, I will cause ruling thrones of iniquity to topple. Like Dagon, their head will fall before My Presence! Get ready! I shake loose wicked structures. Watch in the night and watch Me manifest in the light!

Earlier you read about the three fourteen-generation times aligning. Fourteen is a double seven. The number seven is linked with completion and fulfillment and is the number that the Lord uses to represent the Holy Spirit. The sevenfold Spirit and the candle in the Book of Revelation are important for us to understand in a "Holy Spirit" year: "Directly in front of his throne were seven lighted lamps representing the sevenfold Spirit of God" (Rev. 4:5, TLB). Isaiah 11:2 (NKJV), says, "The Spirit of the LORD shall rest upon Him, the Spirit of wisdom and understanding, the Spirit of counsel and might, the Spirit of knowledge and of the fear of the LORD." Ask the Lord for the Holy Spirit to overpower you during this season. Expect Him not only to move in the cities and nations of the world, but also to visit you personally.

How do we receive revelation from God for our next step in order to move to our next glory manifestation? How do we listen for the voice of God? *Many times these answers come when we receive a visitation from the Holy Spirit.* What I mean by a visitation from God is simply hearing from Him. God does not visit all people in the same way, but visitation is a valid, legitimate part of Christian life. For us to fully possess our inheritance, we need to understand more about visitation and be open to receiving this gift from God in our own lives.

FIVE OBSERVATIONS ON VISITATION

Over time, certain truths about visitation have been impressed upon me. Here are five particular observations that might help us better understand a Holy Spirit visitation:

1. There is a time of visitation.

In the New Testament there are two Greek words for *time*. One is *chronos*, and the other is *kairos*. The word *chronos* refers to chronological time—days, weeks, months, years. *Kairos* refers to an appointed time or an opportune time. For instance when a woman is pregnant, she spends nine months of *chronos* time in pregnancy waiting for her child, but when she goes into labor, the *kairos* time for the birth of her child has come.

The Lord has appointed our *kairos* times that He has set aside for visitation. When speaking prophetically to the city of Jerusalem, Jesus said, "For days will come upon you when your enemies will build an embankment around you, surround you and close you in on every side, and level you, and your children within you, to the ground; and they will not leave in you one stone upon another, because *you did not know the time of your visitation*" (Luke 19:43–44, emphasis added).

In his book *Welcoming a Visitation of the Holy Spirit*, Wesley Campbell says:

> God visited Jerusalem many times. His voice came through His prophets. His glory came in *kairos* events such as the building of the temples. Finally, He came through His Son, Jesus Christ, who boldly stated: "Anyone who has seen me has seen the Father" (John 14:9). However, after only three years of ministry, Jesus was forced to declare that enemies would raze the holy city of Jerusalem to

the ground as judgment for not recognizing Him, even when He came in the flesh (see Luke 19:41–44). The prophesied judgment happened in A.D. 70 when Jerusalem was destroyed by the Roman invader, Titus.[8]

Jerusalem missed her time of visitation and, consequently, could not even recognize the Lord when He stood in the midst. Likewise, if we do not perceive our times of visitation, how would we recognize the Lord if He were to stand in our midst? You must understand that the Lord desires to bring visitation to you, and you must stand ready for your *kairos* time.

2. During times of visitation, miraculous blessings come.

By far the greatest visitation of God in history was during the thirty-three years Jesus walked on Earth. As Jesus moved among the people, tremendous blessings on an unprecedented scale fell on those with whom He came into contact. The blind received sight; the deaf heard; the lame walked; the dead were raised; sin was forgiven; bondages were broken; demoniacs were freed; and death, hell, and the grave were soundly defeated.

As the Lord comes in contact with us today, why should we expect less? Miraculous blessings are a part of *kairos* times of visitation. They are something we should cry out to God for. Consider the story of blind Bartimaeus who, as Jesus was passing by, cried out for Him. (See Mark 10:46–52.) Those around tried to quiet him down, but Bartimaeus shouted louder. Jesus, hearing him cry out, called to Bartimaeus and asked him what he wanted Jesus to do for him. When Bartimaeus asked to receive his sight, Jesus said, "Go your way; your faith has made you well" (v. 52). Bartimaeus recognized the *kairos* time of Jesus's visitation. He also knew that if he did not cry out then, Jesus might not pass by again, and the chance to be healed would be lost.

Like blind Bartimaeus, you too must be ready for your visitation and willing to cry out to God for whatever miraculous blessing you are needing in your own life.

3. Faithfulness and consistency produce surprise visitation.

In Luke 1:5–25 we read the story of the priest Zacharias who was righteous and blameless in the sight of the Lord. He was a good man who followed God's commandments and fulfilled the duties of his priesthood faithfully, but he and his wife, Elizabeth, had no children. Apparently he had petitioned the Lord concerning their barrenness. One day, while performing his normal priestly duties, an angel of the Lord visited him and told him that his petition had been heard and that Elizabeth would bear a son whom they were to name John.

By no biblical indications were Zacharias or Elizabeth extraordinary people. They were a man and woman of God who were found righteous in His sight. They were also faithful and consistent in the portion God had given them. It was in the consistent performance of Zacharias's duties that his *kairos* time of visitation came, and his prayer for a child was answered.

No one can know when a time of visitation is coming, but your faithfulness in serving in the portion God has given you and crying out to God for those barren places in your life can be a catalyst to a visitation—arriving when you least expect to hear from Him.

4. Visitation secures our inheritance.

Job 10:12 (KJV) says, "Thou hast granted me life and favour, and thy visitation hath preserved my spirit." In Hebrew, the word *preserved* in this passage is *shamar*, meaning to guard, keep safe, protect, watch over, or care for. It is the same word used in Genesis 2:15 when Adam was called to tend and keep (*shamar*) the garden. It is also used when God commanded the people of God to guard over the covenant. (See Genesis 17:9; Exodus 31:14; Deuteronomy 28:9.)

Here in Job we see that God has granted life and favor and that His visitation has preserved (*shamared*) Job's spirit. Every time the will of God comes from heaven to Earth and God's glory is present, then our destiny, our inheritance, our very spirit, is guarded, protected, watched over—*shamared*—by the Spirit of God through that visitation. How is that so? When visitation comes, God always releases some type of strategic information that thrusts us forward in His purposes. As we respond to His visitation and to the strategic information we receive, we possess a greater portion of our inheritance. Therefore, as God manifests Himself through visitation, He is *shamaring* His purposes for our lives and securing our inheritance.

5. Visitation produces glory

The true manifest presence of God cannot visit humans without His glory radiating from that presence. At times God does reveal His glory to man visibly, much as He did for me that night in Houston. Such a display of the presence of God is often seen as fire or dazzling light, perhaps as a cloud or mist, or sometimes as an act of His mighty power. Even if we do not visibly see manifestations of His glory, the visitation we experience leaves us with an impression of His glory burned into our hearts. It is, after all, the inward and hidden work in our hearts that produces the Christlike attributes that move us from glory to glory.

This is a time to "trim your wicks," watch, and wait patiently for the Holy Spirit to visit you. Do not be like the *unwise virgins* and lose your expectation of what will happen in days ahead! I am praying for the transforming power and glory of the Holy Spirit to overcome you. Expect His glory to invade your home, workplace, city, state, and nation.

In biblical writings, visitation is linked with the divine investigation or inspection of men's character and deeds. When God visits, it is like an audit review occurs. My pastor is Robert Heidler. His wife, Linda, is a wonderful, prophetic prayer leader and minister. She had the following vision:

> In March of 1997, we were in a Sunday morning church service. I began to have a vision. In this vision, I knew that the Lord was coming to visit my house. I had cleaned everything cleaner than ever before. My carpets were cleaned, my curtains were washed and ironed, and everything was dusted and polished. I had fresh flowers on the table. I could not think of anything else to do to make my house ready for the Lord to come. It was the best it could possibly be.

All at once, the Lord was standing in my house. He had not come to the door; He just appeared. I did not know what to say or to do. He looked around and then pointed to one wall of my living room and said, "That whole wall has to go." I was in shock. That wall was the one between my living room and garage. My washer and dryer were on the other side of that wall. I wanted to protest, but as the Lord spoke the words, the wall shattered. Sheet rock, two-by-fours and wires protruded from the wall, and the room was covered in plaster dust.

Before I could recover from that, the Lord pointed to a room off the back of my house. In reality, I did not have a room like this, only in the vision. This room had all kinds of awards, pictures, trophies, medals, and so on. It also had family heirlooms. The Lord pointed to that room and said, "That whole room has to go." Immediately, I thought of getting all my treasures out, but the Lord said, "And don't try to get anything out, either." As I looked, a huge crane appeared in my backyard and a wrecking ball swung across and demolished the room.

My house was a wreck, I was in shock, and I didn't know what to do. This was not what I had anticipated, but it was very clear that the Lord knew what needed to happen in my house. I love this vision. It speaks for itself. The Lord is saying, *"Even though you've got everything in order, get ready for the changes I am bringing!"*[9]

Ten years later, a tremendous flood came to Denton, Texas, where we all live. While Robert and Linda were on a prayer journey to Ireland and Scotland, this flood devastated their home. When they returned, their beautiful home was in shambles. They could have been devastated. However, they remembered the dream and the word the Lord had given years prior. Instead of falling apart, they drew a new plan of expansion for their home. That is a perfect picture of visitation and how to react.

Visitation does not always mean that things are nice, neat, and in order. Actually, when God visits, He points out changes that need to be made. When we interact with Him, these changes always work for our good.

In a good sense, God visits us with His care, providence, and mercy! "Thy visitation hath preserved my spirit" (Job 10:12, KJV). He is the Father of our spirits and watches after the spirit of man. He visits us so that our spirits will remain renewed, refreshed, and vibrant in Him. If He sees the spirits of His children being vexed, He will visit and redirect our paths so that vexation will not overtake us. Righteous Lot's spirit had been vexed in Sodom and Gomorrah because of the evil that had invaded those cities. God visited and gave Lot and his family an opportunity to leave before He judged the city. In a sense of judgment, sometimes calamity or distress becomes our lot in order to realign us to God's will!

Isaiah 10:3 (KJV) says, "What will ye do in the day of visitation, and in the desolation which shall come from far?" Visitation is God's action of stepping into time and rearranging human affairs. Whether we determine His visitation as a blessing or judgment is usually based upon our earnest love and relationship with Him.

THE DAY OF VISITATION

God has a moment when He comes. We can fail to prepare for that moment. The moment can occur, and we can miss our time of visitation. Luke 19:41–44 says:

> Now as He drew near, He saw the city and wept over it, saying, "If you had known, even you, especially in this your day, the things that make for your peace! But now they are hidden from your eyes. For days will come upon you when your enemies will build an embankment around you, surround you and close you in on every side, and level you, and your children within you, to the ground; and they will not leave in you one stone upon another, because you did not know the time of your visitation.

Jesus had a great emotional release over Jerusalem missing her day of visitation. For three years there had been a preparation and demonstration, and yet they still did not *see* the Redeemer in their midst.

After this passage of Scripture comes the cleansing of the temple. Actually, you can make a correlation between their blindness to visitation and the temple worship in that day. I believe we miss our day of visitation if our corporate worship is not vibrant and filled with the expectancy of the Lord's return.

Visitation also means the numbering of soldiers or the taking of a census. How we cast our vote in times of election is a way that we participate in the government of the future. One of the definitions of visitation is the appointment of a person to an office; therefore, how we vote is linked with visitation. If we do not vote for righteousness, then we will not be visited or ruled righteously.

Visitation occurs when humans are crying out and seeking the Lord for help. If we cry, He will come. Visitation is the manifestation or results of God's involvement with particular persons or groups of people in time of need. God has knowledge of people's concerns and intervenes with His manifest presence. When He renders aid to us He has visited us in our time of need. When visitation comes, favor is released upon us.

> *We miss our day of visitation if our corporate worship is not vibrant and filled with the expectancy of the Lord's return.*

EXPECT VISITATION

You would think that all of us would wake up each day with an expectation that God would come and visit us. However, biblically, you do not see many people ever expecting Him to visit. Expectations are linked with our emotions, as I will discuss in a later chapter. If your expectations are wounded or disappointed, then you will lose the desire and longing for relationship. This causes your heart to harden, guarding your emotions from being hurt again. In so doing, you lose the anticipation of God coming and meeting with you.

After ninety years, Sarah lost the expectation of God coming to visit her. She actually laughed when she was told that she would have a child within a year. God visited her and confronted her laugh. Moses had lost sight of any visitation. He had worked for forty years in the land of Midian and had all but forgotten his prior royal life in the palace of Pharaoh. He did not expect God to visit him in a burning bush; however, he did turn aside to see the bush burn. The next forty years of his life dramatically changed.

Eli did not expect visitation! In 1 Samuel 1–3 we find that Eli's heart had grown very cold. His sons had grown very rebellious. Hannah, a barren woman, cried out for visitation. God visited her with a son, Samuel. She dedicated that child to the Lord and gave him to Eli, a hardened, ungodly priest, to be raised in the temple. The Bible even says that the word of the Lord had become very "rare" in those days. In other words, there was very little revelation or visitation from God. One night, God visited Samuel. Samuel, who did not know the voice of the Lord, went to Eli and questioned why Eli kept calling him. Eli said, "If you hear this voice again, it is the Lord; ask Him what you should do" (1 Sam. 3:9, author's paraphrase). God visited Samuel and gave him a word for Eli. This started a new course of history in Israel. When one generation grows cold in their expectation for visitation, God raises up another generation who can hear.

I have already shared about the people of Jerusalem not expecting their Savior. However, the people closest to Jesus sometimes did not expect Him to come. He had prophesied in Matthew 16 that He would die and be raised three days later. This prophecy was fulfilled very shortly after it was spoken. In the midst of the emotional week of Jesus's death, the disciples forgot the prophecy. In John we find this account:

> Then, the same day at evening, being the first day of the week, when the doors were shut where the disciples were assembled, for fear of the Jews, Jesus came and stood in the midst, and said to them, "Peace be with you." Now when He had said this, He showed them His hands and His side. Then the disciples were glad when they saw the Lord.
>
> —John 20:19–20

Once they saw Him, their emotions began to come alive to His will again. He then said to them again:

> "Peace to you! As the Father has sent Me, I also send you." And when He had said this, He breathed on them, and said to them, "Receive the Holy Spirit. If you forgive the sins of any, they are forgiven them; if you retain the sins of any, they are retained."
> —JOHN 20:21–23

Even in their grief and confusion, the apostles were commissioned by Jesus as the apostles of the future!

When we continue this story, we read about Thomas.

> Now Thomas, called the Twin, one of the twelve, was not with them when Jesus came. The other disciples therefore said to him, "We have seen the Lord." So he said to them, "Unless I see in His hands the print of the nails, and put my finger into the print of the nails, and put my hand into His side, I will not believe." And after eight days His disciples were again inside, and Thomas with them. Jesus came, the doors being shut, and stood in the midst, and said, "Peace to you!" Then He said to Thomas, "Reach your finger here, and look at My hands; and reach your hand here, and put it into My side. Do not be unbelieving, but believing." And Thomas answered and said to Him, "My Lord and my God!" Jesus said to him, "Thomas, because you have seen Me, you have believed. Blessed are those who have not seen and yet have believed."
> —JOHN 20:24–29

Trauma has ways of keeping our expectations of visitation paralyzed. We will discuss more about this later. Jesus will visit. Hopefully we will not be like Thomas, and we will recognize His day of visitation.

CHOOSE YOU THIS DAY

Ecclesiastes 3:10–14 (AMP) says:

> I have seen the painful labor and exertion and miserable business
> which God has given to the sons of men with which to exercise
> and busy themselves. He has made everything beautiful in its time.
> He also has planted eternity in men's hearts and minds [a divinely
> implanted sense of a purpose working through the ages which
> nothing under the sun but God alone can satisfy], yet so that men
> cannot find out what God has done from the beginning to the end.
> I know that there is nothing better for them than to be glad and to
> get and do good as long as they live; and also that every man should
> eat and drink and enjoy the good of all his labor—it is the gift of
> God. I know that whatever God does, it endures forever; nothing
> can be added to it nor anything taken from it. And God does it
> so that men will [reverently] fear Him [revere and worship Him,
> knowing that He is].

Man was made to recognize the moment and understand the power of
choice! The will is an interesting dynamic of man. The will of man must
choose the best God has for him.

The will is linked with our wishes and desires. Jesus only acted in
accordance and in harmony with the will of the heavenly Father (John
5:30; 6:38). Jesus had to choose to lay down His life for us. This released an acceptable day of salvation through eternity. Luke 22:42 says, "Father, if it is Your will, take this cup away from Me; nevertheless not My will, but Yours, be done." A will can also be a written testament of what one chooses to do with their possessions. Because Jesus chose to do Father's will, eternity has been planted in our hearts. We must choose to serve Him daily. We must yield our lives to Him. When we make that choice and align our will with His will, we are assured our day of visitation.

The choices we are making now will release our supply for the future.

THE VALLEY OF DECISION

I recently awakened and heard the words, "Valley of Decision." There is a process occurring in the earth realm that is bringing the winepress to a new place of fullness. We are at *Shechem*, the "place of choice," in church history! This is causing us to choose God's covenant purposes in the earth. How the church chooses is how the conflict of the nations will be determined. How the church makes this choice will release the Lord's inheritance in the earth for this generation.

Most of us are reflecting this place of choice in our personal lives. I see believers making key choices in relationships, positions (both territorial as well as vocational), and ministry alignments. I also see that the choices we are making now will release our supply for the future. Remember, this is a defining year! As I researched this "decision valley" in Joel 3:14, I found that this was the *Valley of Jehoshaphat.* Jehoshaphat had made reforms that had changed the course of his nation, but he was facing his greatest external threat. Not just one enemy but an alliance was coming against him, producing insurmountable odds for victory. His first step was to humble himself in the midst of this great trial. Three elements of spiritual discipline put God's covenant people in a right position for victory: *fasting, prayer,* and *praise*. With these spiritual dynamics working, *prophecy and revelation* could be released so that in this valley, the children of God would emerge victoriously. Their battle was one of praise and worship. God's battle was to dismantle and remove the enemy by dispatching the hosts of heaven. I declare this same scenario over you.

WHEN YOU COME TO YOUR SHECHEM, CHOOSE!

A key place of choice in the Word of God was *Shechem*. In Joshua 24:14–15, at the end of Joshua's time of leadership, he admonished the people to "put away the gods which your fathers served on the other side of the River. . . . Serve the LORD! And if it seems evil to you to serve the LORD, choose for yourselves this day whom you will serve, whether the gods which your fathers served...or the gods of the Amorites, in whose land you dwell. But as for me and my house, we will serve the LORD!" Shechem was located in the valley between Mount Ebal and Mount Gerizim. It provided a large, natural amphitheater for a gathering of all the tribes. In Joshua 8:30–35, we see that this place was the spiritually significant defining place of meeting before they went in to fully possess the land. The invincible place of Jericho had been overcome, and the mistake of Ai had been rectified. They had utterly destroyed everything in Ai and all the inhabitants of Ai, and the spoil of that city would be their supply to advance. Then Joshua worshiped and renewed God's covenant. He read all the words of the Law, the blessings and the curses. The people gathered in this beautiful valley and heard this being shouted from one mountain to the other antiphonally. They heard it perfectly; there was no confusion in their hearing.

The first step in making our choice is to stop and worship God. Exalt Him for your key victories, and thank Him for His grace even in your past mistakes. As we present ourselves to God without reserve and empty ourselves before Him, we can clearly hear without confusion the choice He has before us. Confusion is always linked with a spirit of Babylon, where the devil has authored a structure filled with deception. The Lord desires to bring your heart and mind to a place of peace. *Peace* means wholeness. *There are three generations now standing at Shechem!* They are listening carefully to the choice that is before them. This day is filled with *blessings* or *curses*!

The blood of our Savior can deliver us from the curse and cause us to enter into the eternal blessings in heavenly places (Eph. 1:3). However, we must look through the confusion of mammon and Babylon to make the correct choice at this time. When we hear the choice of our blessing, God writes the boundaries of that choice upon our heart. The power of His Spirit allows us to move freely by grace within those boundaries. If we will make *His presence* our central theme, the voice of blessing will become louder than the voice of cursing. If we choose blessing, then the events of the world will line up with the choice of God's people. When we align ourselves with the Head, the manifestation of that choice will set the course in the earth realm. The Lord is opening His *treasure* in heaven based upon this choice that His people are making. Activate your will NOW and align it with God's so that the confusion that is occurring in the world will not cause you to shake but will cause you to stand steady in the midst of the war ahead. Watch the next generation receive the benefits and results of this choice.

How Long Will You Be Halted Between Two Opinions?

Elijah was in a contest on Mount Carmel with the prophets of Baal. This was to determine who was Lord of the region. The people were double minded. Through circumstances, God was bringing them to a place of choice, but they kept going back and forth between God's worship and the confusion linked with Baal's revelation in their society. God defied all human reasoning at this point. It was Elijah against the four hundred fifty—impossible odds in the natural, yet nothing was impossible with the Lord. The people needed to get "unhalted"!

To *halt* means to walk with a limp or become lame; to stand in doubt between two courses or paths; to display weakness or imperfection; to put things on hold; to cease marching or journeying; to discontinue or terminate a project for lack of funds. Again on Mount Carmel, worship became the turning point. Elijah built an altar in the name of the Lord and allowed the "river of God" to flow. Then the fire from heaven fell. This caused the people to see that "God, the Lord, He is God!" (1 Kings 18:39). In this choice, we must be willing to confront our enemies and to worship in the midst of our enemies. We must also demonstrate God's power in such a way that a religious world that has only seen a form of godliness and denied the power thereof will have no doubt that we must have supernatural help and intervention at this time in history.

Shift NOW! How to Choose the Lord at This Crossroads of History

Shift! A *shift* is a change of place, position, or direction. A shift also includes an exchange or replacement of one thing for another. A shift is a change of gear so you accelerate. A shift can also be an underhanded or deceitful scheme. Therefore, in our shift we must recognize that the enemy is plotting to stop it. A shift also entails a scheduled time. *Shaking occurs during a shift.* Think of a fault line. To *shift* means a change in frequency. *God is ready for us to shift. Shift with Him!* I am praying that you make this divine shift!

1. *Develop His mind.* Don't lean on your own understanding. You will never make the right choice with your limited knowledge. Philippians 2:5–8 says, "Let this mind be in you which was also in Christ Jesus, who…made Himself of no reputation, taking the form of a bondservant.…He humbled Himself and became obedient." Romans 12:2 says, "Do not be conformed to this world, but be transformed by the renewing of your mind, that you may prove what is that good and acceptable and perfect will of God." This simply means that you shouldn't let Satan's scheme accustom you to the thinking of the world. Also, don't let outward appearances deceive you, causing you to miss what God is doing. We must prove the voice of God and practice in everyday life what God's will from heaven is declaring to us. Romans 8:7 says, "The carnal mind is enmity against God." Declare that the Lord will put His finger on every area of carnality in your thinking.

2. *Learn to express His heart.* Prophecy is expressing the mind and heart of God. Let the Lord deal with your emotions so that they do not cloud you in communicating His heartbeat. Declare that all self-pity and hope deferred is being removed from you. Allow bitterness and unforgiveness to

leave so that you can express what God is thinking. Don't let inordinate affection cause you to misalign your priorities. The heart can have weights or attachments. I declare a "free" heart over you.

3. *Change your atmosphere!* Speak faith! Jesus could do very little in Nazareth because the atmosphere was so filled with unbelief. Jesus was the all-powerful God walking the earth, capable of signs and wonders, yet the atmosphere created a barrier for intervention. Break the negative atmospheric presence around you by prophetic declarations of victory.

4. *Do exploits! Optimize resources!* Remember, this is a year to optimize. That means to see things from a positive standpoint. Daniel 11:32 says, "The people who know their God shall prove themselves strong and shall stand firm and do exploits [for God]" (AMP). To do exploits means to take the resources you have and create new resources or bring them into a new level of fullness. This is one of the things that God means when He says to optimize resources.

5. *Watch for the "suddenlies!"* We've heard about the suddenlies happening, but now we will begin to see them. If hope deferred and weariness are ruling you, you will miss it when God moves on your behalf. If fear is influencing you, you won't understand when God starts breaking through on your behalf. The process that you've been going through is moving toward a suddenly.

6. *Learn the process of going "over"!* This is a season when we must have an "over" mentality. Overtake or be overtaken. Overthrow or be overthrown. Overturn or be overturned. Overcome or be overcome. Be sure you are being overseen. Also, define the sphere that you are overseeing!

7. *Develop a kingdom mentality.* The kingdom of God is within you. We build the church, but we get keys to the kingdom. Study the kingdom. Matthew 11:12 says, "...now the kingdom of heaven suffers violence, and the violent take it by force." The kingdom advances in victory. This occurs through violent spiritual conflict and warfare. God used John the Baptist and Elijah to teach us to move forward. Fear not! The church is God's warring agent. Worship and war! The kingdom increases. Understand the sword and the fire because they are both important in the battle ahead.

Ask Him to visit you. Wake up each day with an expectation of meeting and communing with Him. Your times are in His hands.

CHAPTER 5

FROM ONE NARROW TRANSITION TO ANOTHER: A KINGDOM ON THE MOVE

WE ARE A PEOPLE ON THE MOVE. WE ARE MOVING OUR RESI-dences from one place to another. We are moving from one work position to another. Many even change vocations in life. Life has many passages that we must face with faith and courage. The body of Christ goes through these same phases of growth, maturity, and change. Transition is a word that helps us understand these changes. Many of you, like me, have been through so many transitions in your life that you could write this book as well as I. We could venture to say that we are experts in transitions, but every transition is different and entails a different set of circumstances and events. Therefore, each transition has a time element and a narrow place that becomes very dangerous for us to navigate through. Just remember that we all go through transitions, but you must end one and begin another to keep moving into your next place or else you will remain mired in your present transition, and it will become your future.

At every transition, we cross over!

WHAT IS A TRANSITION?

A *transition* is a passage from one state, stage, subject, or place to another. Transitions occur because there has come a necessary time for *change* in a movement. By evolving from one form, stage, or style to another, new developments occur in our life processes. Transitions can also entail abrupt changes in energy states or levels accompanied by loss or gain of a single quantum of energy. Energy is linked with work and power, so transitions affect our work.

At every transition, we cross over! Remember how we shared that Abraham the Hebrew was one who crossed over. If we are grafted into the Abrahamic covenant through the blood of Jesus, then we are a people who are always crossing over. Each phase of transition is a transition in itself. In order to move across to occupy our inheritance, we must come to an ending or death of one phase of our life. We must let go of one thing to embrace something new. We are a people who do not like to die. Therefore, we usually hang on with all of our strength to something in a phase of our life that is ending instead of gracefully releasing one good thing for something better.

When we are unwilling to understand and receive teaching in our processes that are producing change in our lives, then we fall into the category of being ignorant.

A normal phase of transition is the confusion phase. To move to a new place we must allow our mind to embrace new ways, methods, and understandings. When new revelation is coming into our mind, we seem confused at times because we have not fully replaced our old cognitive processes. Therefore the last season's ideas are warring with this season's revelation. We are not clear exactly how to advance until we get the next piece of the puzzle that helps our vision unfold.

In the next chapter, I will discuss another phase of transition: the pain phase of change. Leaving behind the old can be painful, and at times we have to face pain to advance. However, in every process we must remember that the best is yet ahead and that the process of transition we are in will produce a new beginning.

BEWARE OF THREE KINDS
OF IGNORANCE

We can perish because of lack of knowledge. In every transition, we must be willing to receive the revelation that the Lord has for us to cross over into the new. Ignorance is synonymous with being simple, naïve, or acting foolishly. When we are unwilling to understand and receive teaching in our processes that are producing change in our lives, then we fall into ignorance. Ignorance can mean that we have rejected knowledge, causing us to lack perception and discernment. *Not knowing* something that is necessary for our advancement is termed ignorance in a facet of the change cycle we are in. This results in a lack of success and causes us to *err* or *go astray*. The sin of *ignorance* of God's Word cannot be used as an excuse at certain times in our life; if we refuse knowledge and revelation, we refuse growth and maturity.

Paul used the phrase, "I do not want you to be ignorant" (Rom. 11:25, NIV), when he was leading the body to understand the power of forgiveness and how the enemy uses our lack of forgiveness to create schemes that overcome us. He also used this phrase when teaching the Corinthians about spiritual gifts (1 Cor. 12:1). *Ignorance* is linked with disobedience and therefore causes us to reject God's way and each other along the way. Ignorance can be unintentional, but it usually results from hardening our hearts against an idea or change of God.

Ignorance has three categories. The first is *indolence*, or being dull, unfeeling, or barren. The result of this is laziness, hastiness, presumption, and poverty. Another manifestation that can reveal you have fallen into this category is procrastination. When we fall into passivity, we stop advancing into the purposes of God for our life.

The next category is *keenness*. If you feel as if you *know it all*, you become unteachable. Then you are unable to move into the new thing that God has for you. One downfall of religion is the thought that you know all about God and He cannot do anything outside the box of knowledge that you have created. This leads us to conceit, and the pride of this knowledge puffs us up and positions us for a fall. Keenness will also lead us into passivity and complacency. We believe that we know it all (Job 32:13).

The most dangerous area of ignorance is *no illumination*. The word of the Lord becomes *rare*. In our disobedience, the Lord quits communing with us on a daily basis. Daily turns into weekly, which turns into yearly. Then we enter a season of silence. This is very dangerous because "where there is no vision [or prophetic utterance], the people perish" (Prov. 29:18, KJV).

Transitions Are Characterized by Shifts in Sound

Another definition of *transition* is a shift in sound or a musical modulation, or a passage leading from one section of a piece to another. Sound creates movement. Worship and sound are important. Open the window and receive the sound of the Lord! Let the wind of the Spirit bring the sound that you need through the window of heaven and into the place where you are standing.

Your conscience is like a window between soul and spirit. Make sure nothing is clouding your conscience. Sound that leads you into movement and worship will cause your conscience to remain in alignment with God. The conscience is one of the absolute authorities of our life. When our conscience is aligned and interacting with the Word of God, the "window" remains clean and open. The conscience is the lamp of the body. The conscience is the eye of our spirit that causes us to see into the heavenly realms.

We say what we see! Open your mouth and release the decree that is in your heart! This is the season of confession and decree. What we say now determines our future. If we will cleanse our conscience, then the revelation that has not been able to influence our minds will find entrance.

Let the shout of the Lord arise in you. Let your confidence in the Lord be heard. Though the enemy is roaming like a mighty lion, seeking whom he may destroy, there is a *roar* in you to be released at this time. This roar will defy the enemy. Go past that which seems invincible in your life. Get in the river of change that is flowing by your door and let it take you to your next place. Get a shield of protection around you, and birth the *new* that the Lord has for you. Your latter end (future) will be greater than your beginning!

CHANGE YOUR PERSPECTIVE

Sometimes things aren't what they seem. They may look a certain way, but when we see them from a different angle, they are completely different. *Perspective* is a glass through which an object is viewed. When you see something, you draw what you perceive on a plane surface. *Perspective* can be a true resemblance of an object or of how the object is perceived by the eye. When several objects are grouped together, or we have several situations in our life happening at one time, we are impressed by what we see and gain knowledge so we better observe how to walk in the situations that are confronting us.

When our conscience is aligned and interacting with the Word of God, the "window" remains clean and open.

We are affected by all the stimuli and emotional aspects of these situations. This can cloud how we actually "see" the world around us. A *perspective* can also be a kind of painting that you see in gardens and at the end of a gallery. The landscape or alley can actually be altered by the painting itself. Recently in a prayer meeting, I heard the Lord say, "My people have lost their perspective. Therefore, they are losing reality!" John Dickson and I began to sing and write the following song, "I See a Light."[1]

> I see a light—at the end of my darkness
> A light—like a brush on a canvas
> Splashing new colors on me
> Colors I never could see.

I see a light—shining out of the dark
And I rise—and push myself forward
Shaky at first as I try
'Cause my eyes still aren't used to this light
And I've been here since Lord knows when.

My wounds and fears kept me locked up within
And I couldn't open up and couldn't forgive!
But I hear my Shepherd calling me
Just like Lazarus when he got free
And I know this love can roll the stone away!

But I see a light—at the end of my darkness
A light—like a brush on a canvas
Splashing new colors on me colors I never could see
I see a light! I see a light! I see a light!

Our life is like a canvas with an ever-changing perspective and horizon line. What at first seems very large and unconquerable actually is not once we get into the position to see it from the standpoint of reality. Usually, our problem is just *out of perspective*. The enemy has to make us reason that our looming problem is a larger foe than it actually is. He attempts to determine our perspective. We must learn to stand back and refocus on our canvas of life and determine both our horizon line and perspective.

In *One Thing: How to Keep Your Faith in a World of Chaos*, Pam and I write several stories about grabbing hold of reality.[2] Those *simple things* are what usually show us true value. They create a faith dimension that we can touch. They even have us touch eternity, which is reality. I actually think most of us are searching for reality. I also believe that only by touching the One who created reality can we find and distinguish between what is truly helpful or detrimental to us in the long run.

In Pam's first pregnancy, she had many troubling experiences. Actually, we were living in some very hard circumstances that were trying to overwhelm our life. In *One Thing* I share:

I had changed our assignment and moved from being on a church staff to serving at a boys and girls home. There were 100 young people who had problems, a staff with problems, and an organization that seemed to have problems. On top of this, our long-awaited promise of bearing a child had become a reality, yet now we were hearing about all these health problems that could happen to the child as she was knit together in Pam's womb. Additionally, there were financial problems. I was in a walk of faith over finances. We had received a notice from the IRS that I owed some money after leaving my secular job, and we had doctor bills, and so on. And on top of this, Pam had lost the use of her left arm during her sickness. I'm telling you—it was a mess!

One night I felt overwhelmed by the world's circumstances. I made a list of everything that was overwhelming me. I looked at the list that had seven major categories and felt totally overwhelmed. I laid the list aside and went ahead and completed the next day's duties and issues. Later that night I could not rest. Therefore, after Pam went to bed, I took my list and went outside in the field and sat before the Lord. Prayer can take different forms. I knew that the only way I could make it through all of these issues was for the Lord to somehow intervene in my life. I held the list up to the Lord and said, "Read this list!" I knew the Lord understood all the issues on the list, but it was like I just needed Him to see what was bombarding me at this point.

I am sure some of you reading this have felt this way. I then said to the Lord, "What is it that You would have me do with all of this?" And I sat there. By this time, it was around 11:30 p.m., and I wondered if I was going to sit out in the field all night. A few moments later I felt a very clear impression. I heard that wonderful voice say, "Buy your wife a new dress." Now, I only had sixty-seven dollars in our bank account. But I knew His voice. This was the Thursday before Easter. I knew I was not working on Friday, so I took my list and wrote at the bottom of it what the Lord had asked me to do. The next morning I told Pam that we were going to go shopping to buy her a new dress. She questioned me for a moment, but then I said, "It's just what we are supposed to do." We went and bought a new dress, on sale. We then had lunch at a cafeteria and came home. I had two dollars left. Therefore, when the offering plate was passed on Sunday, I just threw those two dollars into the plate and said, "Lord, me and my list are now Yours."

It was amazing what happened next. I looked up in the midst of the choir where my wife sang. While the preacher was preaching, I saw someone throw their hand up in the air. It was Pam! This was not a place that you would have thought a person would be having a spiritual experience of overwhelming praise. The message was not that moving. In fact, it was sort of boggy. On the way home after church I said to Pam, "What were you doing throwing your hand up in the midst of that awful sermon?" (Biblically, the Bible tells us to raise our hands and praise the Lord.) I did not see any reason for praise.

Pam said to me, "During the service I reached down to pull up my pantyhose and the Spirit of God touched me and healed my arm!" THIS WAS ON MY LIST! She continued, "I could do nothing but throw my arm up!" I countered, "But the message was so awful. The pastor was even sharing how healing was not in the atonement." She promptly said, "I am sure glad that God didn't listen to his message." The Lord had read my list and heard my prayer. My wife had entered into praise in the midst of all the chaos and within the next six months, EVERYTHING ON THE LIST was taken care of. All it took was for me to do the one thing the Lord asked me to do: *buy my wife a new dress.*[3]

Faith requires action. What we see by faith is reality. Usually, the complicated things around us bind us to a wrong thought process. Belief is linked with faith, which is linked with glory, which is linked with reality. In the Western world, we really do not see the glory realm as reality. We can only access this realm by faith. Faith requires action from us—some sort of response. Let me say it this way: all it really takes is performing one simple faith action to experience reality, and all of the complexities of the world around you begin to dissipate!

When I tell my wife what the enemy is saying or showing me, she always says, "If it is the enemy, why are you listening and looking?" Several years ago I got very sick and experienced a time of great infirmity. The problems were centered around my esophagus and colon. Eventually, in the midst of this time of sickness, I could not eat for several days. I had grown allergic to anything that would enter my body, and each stimulus would result in an anaphylactic shock. I was visiting doctors two to three times a day and chose to just drink water, which seemed safe. On the nineteenth day of this water-only forced fast, the enemy spoke to me and said, "You will never eat again." The enemy's voice is very strong in our time of weakness.

I was lying on the floor and visibly shaken by this spiritual demonic assault. Pam came through our living room and asked me what the problem was. In my self-pity I said, "Other than I am dying, the enemy told me I would never be able to eat again." With great compassion she asked me to walk back to our bedroom with her. I just knew she was going to pray with me.

As we walked through the hall of our home, we passed by our children's bedrooms. At this time, our only daughter, Rebekah, was living with us. In her room was a full length mirror. Pam stood me in front of the mirror and said, "Now tell me what you see." I looked in the mirror and saw myself. She said, "That is reality!" She then made a statement that changed my whole perspective. She exclaimed, "I don't know how long the Lord will not let you eat in the midst of this sickness you are involved in. However, if you will just look in the mirror, we really do not have to worry about becoming anemic for at least a couple of years." After laughing and enjoying the moment, I realized how the enemy's voice had tried to jar me out of my stability and cause me to miss the reality of what God was doing.

When Israel would come before the Lord in times of trouble they would begin by putting things in their proper perspective. They would publicly tell the great things that God had done for them in the past. Jehoshaphat did this when he was faced with impending destruction from an approaching army. He brought the nation together and began to determine the perspective.

> Are You not our God, who drove out the inhabitants of this land before Your people Israel, and gave it to the descendants of Abraham Your friend forever? And they dwell in it, and have built You a sanctuary in it for Your name, saying, "If disaster comes upon us— sword, judgment, pestilence, or famine—we will stand before this temple and in Your presence (for Your name is in this temple), and cry out to You in our affliction, and You will hear and save." And now, here are the people of Ammon, Moab, and Mount Seir....
>
> —2 CHRONICLES 20:7–10

By the time they got to their request, their perspective was changed. They were no longer a doomed people but a people who served a mighty God. I have found in every circumstance that if I begin to praise and proclaim the goodness of God, and if I submit myself to God, draw near to Him, and resist the enemy, then he will flee!

John Dickson says, "*Tehillah*, or the Hebrew word for praise, is not to be confused with the Mexican liquor that has a similar name. That will cause movement, but nothing like praising God!"[4] *Tehillah* means to praise a certain quality or deed that is deserving of praise. Other Hebrew words focus on thanksgiving or actions like kneeling, raising our hands, celebrating, dancing, and so forth, but *tehillah* focuses on declaring the attributes of God or the things He has done. When we do that, His vision enters our vision and the perspective from which we are seeing things changes. This produces many of the transitions that we find ourselves confronting. This changes our perspective of our enemy as well. Satan might have made a certain problem look huge, but we begin to minimize what we have magnified by recounting all the wonderful things that God has already done for us. We begin proclaiming His faithfulness and power. Soon that problem, which seemed so enormous, becomes manageable. David says in Psalm 34:3, "Oh, magnify the LORD."

Sound can come in the form of a report, which is why we must choose whose report we will receive.

Why Would We Need
to Magnify the Lord?

When our problems seem to overwhelm us, the problem is not God's size. Rather, the problem is our perspective if we allow Him to decrease in the midst of our increasing circumstances. When that happens, we need to magnify the Lord and put Him back in His proper perspective. To magnify can also be to amplify. *Magnify* means to make great or greater or to increase the apparent dimensions of something. To *magnify* can mean to make great in representation as you praise and exalt the description of something or someone.

Psalm 149, one of my favorite passages, reads:

> Praise the Lord! Sing to the Lord a new song, praise Him in the assembly of His saints! Let Israel rejoice in Him, their Maker; let Zion's children triumph and be joyful in their King! Let them praise His name in chorus and choir and with the [single or group] dance; let them sing praises to Him with the tambourine and lyre! For the Lord takes pleasure in His people; He will beautify the humble with salvation and adorn the wretched with victory.
>
> Let the saints be joyful in the glory and beauty [which God confers upon them]; let them sing for joy upon their beds. Let the high praises of God be in their throats and a two-edged sword in their hands, to wreak vengeance upon the nations and chastisement upon the peoples, to bind their kings with chains, and their nobles with fetters of iron, to execute upon them the judgment written. He [the Lord] is the honor of all His saints. Praise the Lord! (Hallelujah!)
>
> —Psalm 149:1–9, amp

We magnify the Lord with our mouths. The praises that come from our hearts flood out of our mouths, and the sound of those praises is very sharp. They overtake the enemy's structure. The sound of God's order being declared by His people penetrates and divides our soul and spirit (Heb. 4:12). The sound of God flowing through His people, stirring up His river that is deep within our bellies, is like rushing water that overtakes the atmosphere around us (Rev. 1:15). If we will praise God on the high places of the enemies that have attempted to overtake us throughout the generations, we will see iniquitous, idolatrous patterns in our life overcome.

THRONE ROOM SOUNDS PRODUCE KINGDOM MOVEMENT

In *The Worship Warrior: Ascending in Worship, Descending in War*, I share the importance of heaven's sound.

> A physical sound has always led the armies of God forth. I always visualize it this way: God is on His throne, and Jesus is seated next to Him. Jesus is the door that we have into the Father's throne room. The Word of God tells us in James 5 to submit ourselves to God, draw near to Him, and then resist the devil. I believe that as we worship and submit ourselves to a holy God, we can come into intimate contact with Him. Even though we walk here on the earth in our worshipful submission, we ascend into heaven. As we individually seek God and ascend into the throne room, we can hear the sound in heaven in our spirit man on Earth.
>
> God always led His people forth with sound. We find in Numbers 10 that trumpets would sound. We also find this all the way through the book of Revelation. The book of Revelation is just an incredible, elaborate pageant that is interpreted to us by heavenly, celestial singers along with creatures and elders. John saw a door standing open in heaven, and the voice he heard was like a trumpet speaking and saying, "Come up here and I will show you things that must take place after this" (see Rev. 1:10). The Lord's voice many times sounds like a trumpet calling us forth. The trumpet, or shofar, in the Word of God had a distinct sound to assemble and call God's people to war. Another sound we find before God led His troops forward was "the wind in the mulberry trees." In 2 Samuel 5, David had experienced a major breakthrough in his own life. What had been prophesied over him 29 years prior had actually come into fulfillment. He then had to lead the armies forth into battle. David

had one driving purpose: to get the Ark of the Covenant of God back into its rightful position in the midst of God's covenant people. When the Philistines heard that David had been anointed as king, they rose up against him. David defeated and drove them back out of his jurisdictional authority. However, they regrouped and started coming back at him again. He then asked the Lord if he was to pursue them. In 2 Samuel 5:24 the Lord answers, "And...when you hear the sound of the marching in the tops of the mulberry trees, then you shall advance quickly." The sound of marching is not just the wind blowing the tops of the trees, but it is the hosts of heaven and the armies of God rustling the leaves and signifying they were present to help David in victory. In the book of Revelation, we find the real issue is relationship between the sounds of heaven and the demonstration of God on Earth. Sound leads us forth.[5]

Only God can reveal Himself to us by His Spirit (Matt. 16). Once we receive revelation, we should begin praying that revelation so that we can move from praying to saying. Prophetic declaration is very important if we want to change the atmosphere of the heavenlies. We become the trumpet of the Lord in the earth. We are that human shofar.

THE BLAST OF THE TRUMPET

In the Old Testament, the blowing of trumpets heralded the Lord's descent. This sound had great power to jar what seemed invincible. Once during worship John Dickson, the minister of music with whom I work, began to do an old song in a new way. He sang "Joshua Fit de Battle of Jericho." There is no better biblical example of the sound of tearing down our powerful foe than that of Joshua leading the armies of God against Jericho. As John sang this song, faith

Only God can reveal Himself to us by His Spirit.

began to rise in the people. Not only did we give an incredible shout that shook the heavens, but the many shofars in the conference came forward and began to blow. Great faith was released.

In *The Worship Warrior*, John Dickson and I wrote, "The trumpet sound preceded the movement of God's presence. This sound warned of approaching danger. This sound was a call to arms. This sound meant that redemptive purposes were going to manifest. We find in the book of Revelation that as the trumpet sounded, there had to be a response."[6]

SOUND—"CAUSE TO BE HEARD"

When you look up the word *sound* in Hebrew, you find it is a catalyst needed to make things happen. In the following paragraphs you will find some of the Hebraic uses of our word *sound*. We've already discussed the blowing of the trumpet. Joel 2:1 says, "Sound an alarm!" I like the concept of creating a sound by a "mutter through their throat" that we find in Psalm 115:7. The Father's intentions are always communicated by sound. His voice comes forward, and we know His will. Faith comes by hearing, and hearing by the Word of the Lord. When we come into agreement with God's sound from heaven, whether it be with each other or just with Him, we find a *sumfonia* is produced.

There are many sounds throughout the Bible. When we *yadah*, we confess that Yahweh exists. When we *hallel*, we bring the wind of heaven through our spirit man, releasing into the earth realm His spirit, which affirms and renews our relationship with God. When we *tehillah*, we dance, and then we can also sing songs of deliverance in the midst of the dance. I believe the Lord is taking us into a place of *hillulim*, which is festal jubilation. Sounds will accompany each of these phases as we move forward. How we release sound will be related to how quickly we make it through the transitions we are confronted with.

Sound is voice. The word *phone*, which I think any of us can figure out, is the transference of sound. The trumpet was such an important instrument because of the sound it produced (Exod. 19:19; Josh. 6:5, 20). However, in the Word of God we find sound linked with marching (2 Sam. 5:24). There was a sound of wings that the prophet Ezekiel heard (Ezek. 1:24; 3:13). Daniel heard the sound of the horn (Dan. 3:5, 7). Sound can come in the form of a report (Heb. 12:19). That is why we must choose whose report we will receive. The spies in Numbers 14 gave an evil report. This caused a forty-year delay of God's purposes. Sound is linked to our mouths (Amos 6:5). What we declare from our mouth is also linked with our heart. Logically, then, we can understand that our heart carries a sound. Sound becomes noise when it is confused and cannot be fully interpreted. In Acts 2, there was a sound of a mighty wind. Finally, sound produces soundness. When we are listening to the right sound, we become very sound in our movement. This is why we must learn to praise God with our mouths.

PRAISE CONNECTS US WITH GOD

Why do we praise God? One reason is that God tells us 791 times in the Bible (NIV) to praise, sing, rejoice, celebrate, and dance before Him. Then, of course, there are the demonstrations of shouting, leaping, waving, or clapping our hands. These are not suggestions or even requests. The King of kings, the Leader of the kingdom to which we belong, commands us to demonstrate our allegiance to Him by acts of praise. In his book *Exploring Worship*, Bob Sorge has an interesting take on this: "'Why does God demand our praise?' You may ask, 'Is He some sort of egomaniac who feeds off our adulation?' No, it is not that God needs our praise...He is God, whether we choose to praise Him or not. God has commanded praise for our own good. Not until we praise Him are we able to come into proper relationship with Him."[7]

God does not *need* our praise—He *inhabits* our praise. He moves with our praise. When we praise God, we connect with Him and

> *The impetus of praise is belief in God. The more we believe in God, the more we will praise Him. Those who do not believe in God have no reason to praise Him. To the extent that we acknowledge His sovereign work in our lives, to that degree will our praise ascend.[8]*
> *—Don McMinn*

come into our proper relationship. He is our God, our Father, our Savior, our Deliverer, and "Every good thing given and every perfect gift is from above, coming down from the Father of lights" (James 1:17, NASU). Praise gives us a way to express the gratitude in our hearts and keep our minds focused on Him.

Praise can change any atmospheric warfare around us. Praise can break us out of dry and wilderness times in our lives. The power of our voices with the breath of His Spirit will break the conformity of the enemy's blueprint of the world around us. We often forget that God is our help, our provision, and our healer. If we grow distant in our relationship with our Father, we can draw near to Him, and He to us, through praise and worship. That is why God has to tell us 791 times to praise, rejoice, celebrate, and dance before Him. We forget. We get too busy. The enemy distracts us. We get resisted. Then we get disconnected! Submit yourself to God and praise Him to gain the sound you need to move ahead on the path He has for you. Paul tells us, "Rejoice in the Lord *always*" (Phil. 4:4, emphasis added). This is what keeps us connected and moving with God.

PRAISE CHANGES THE ATMOSPHERE

God tells us to praise not only so that we can express our hearts of gratitude to Him, but also so that we can change our mind-sets, which sometimes become a detriment to us. Have you ever walked around under a *cloud* of discouragement? Instead of your heart being filled with praise, you sense a heaviness, sinking spiritual force, oppression, or depression. You begin to confess, "This is not the day the Lord has made, but this is an awful day!" Think of your worst situation and then remember Job. He arose, tore his robe, and shaved his head; then he fell to the ground and worshiped, and he said: "Naked I came from my mother's womb, and naked shall I return there. The LORD gave, and the LORD has taken away; blessed be the name of the LORD" (Job 1:20–21). His praise led him to a powerful confession: "Though He slay me, yet will I trust Him" (Job 13:15).

About twenty-six hundred years ago, the prophet Habakkuk found himself in a very difficult situation, even worse than most we find ourselves facing. He had obediently prophesied the coming of the Babylonians to bring God's judgment on Judah. As the Babylonians invaded, he would still be living in the area. Sometimes the Lord does not remove us from the judgment around us but keeps us in the midst of what is happening. The very atmosphere over Habakkuk and his nation was filled with despair and dread. Habakkuk began to strengthen himself in the Lord. He began to praise, though there was no reason for him to praise, nor was there any inspiration. He could not say, "Thank You, God, for the good things You have promised me," nor could he exclaim, "Thank You for the excellent future You have prepared for me."

In our darkest moments, we must begin to praise, and we are assured of a victorious end.

All the things we would embrace and draw near to comfort and motivate us today were not available for him. His will had to make a choice to praise God anyway. Habakkuk 3:17–19 gives us the determined tribute that he ended up offering to God.

> Though the fig tree may not blossom,
> Nor fruit be on the vines;
> Though the labor of the olive may fail,
> And the fields yield no food;
> Though the flock may be cut off from the fold,
> And there be no herd in the stalls—
> Yet I will rejoice in the LORD,
> I will joy in the God of my salvation.
>
> The LORD God is my strength;
> He will make my feet like deer's feet,
> And He will make me walk on my high hills.

For Habakkuk, the atmosphere changed. The nation might have had a foreboding cloud over it, but over Habakkuk there was a bright light. His joy was in the Lord. God would give him feet like a deer so that he could walk upon the *high places* in the midst of whatever was happening below. Then, as if realizing what he had just done, he added at the end of the prophecy, "To the Chief Musician. With my stringed instruments." This was an instruction that was normally contained in the subtitles of the psalms, which were given to tell the choir director the instrument the psalm was to be played on and what melody to sing. Only when Habakkuk was finished with this declaration did he realize that he had just written a psalm of praise.

This is a picture of what happens in most of our lives and the reason why we do not continue moving forward through our narrow places and dire straits of life. Sometimes when we begin praising, especially in a very difficult situation, we don't realize what end our powerful praise will bring. In our darkest moments, we must begin, for we are assured of a victorious end.

Hillsong's Darlene Zschech shares the "behind the scenes" of how she wrote one of her most memorable songs:

> "Shout to the Lord" is a song that is popular all over the world. But for me, it was a very expensive song to write. It came out of a personally hard time and it was something that cost me dearly. It cost a lot of my own life. On the wrong side of breakthrough it was too expensive. But on the right side of breakthrough, actually becoming the overcomer, I wouldn't trade it for anything. But just before the wall, it was way too expensive. My inner man couldn't afford it, but something rose up within me…it wasn't me, it was the Spirit of God that made me push through, and on the other side, it was the greatest investment.[9]

PRAISE RELEASES FAITH

When we murmur and complain, it obviously does not release faith. It releases bitterness and hopelessness. Unfortunately, there is nothing more natural for us humans to do than murmur and complain. We are good at it. We don't have to be trained in the art of it. Little children can do it as soon as they learn to talk. If anyone did need lessons, however, the ancient Israelites would be the people to see. They were masters of it. They elevated it to an art form. God could bless their socks off one day, and the next day they would forget all about it and start murmuring and complaining again. The result was that when it came time for them to step out in faith on the edge of their Promised Land, they balked. They had no faith to step out. Their murmuring and complaining had shriveled their faith, and when they needed it the most, it was not there for them.

Paul encourages us in his letter to the Corinthians: "Now all these things happened to them as examples, and they were written for our admonition, on whom the ends of the ages have come" (1 Cor. 10:11).

Praise the Lord! We don't have to suffer the same end as the children of Israel, who were forced to turn their backs on their inheritance and wander in the wilderness for forty years while God raised up a new generation that would rise up in faith and enter in to all the promises that the former generation had forfeited by their murmuring and complaining.

When we develop a lifestyle of praise, it builds our faith so that when we are called upon to step out in faith, it's there for us. We have to maintain our praise. We have to keep clearing the atmosphere over us and determining our own perspective. This is a mission that requires vigilance. Psalm 71:6 says "My praise shall be *continually* of You" (emphasis added). Luke tells us that the early church was "*continually* in the temple praising and blessing God" (Luke 24:53, emphasis added). The writer of Hebrews says, "Therefore by Him let us *continually* offer the sacrifice of praise to God, that is, the fruit of our lips, giving thanks to His name" (Heb. 13:15–16, emphasis added).

When we do this, our faith becomes strong, and God is pleased with us (Heb. 11:6). When God saw Abraham's faith, He was pleased. Abraham's faith was counted as righteousness (Rom. 4:9). God will be pleased with our faith as we build it up through our praise. Robert Gay makes this statement:

> Praise is one of the weapons God has given us. It is not a carnal weapon but a spiritual weapon of war. God is restoring the

123

tabernacle of David today. He is restoring the priestly ministry of praise, and we are to enter into it "so that [we] may possess." It is so that we, the church, may drive out our enemy, the devil, and receive our rightful inheritance.[10]

PRAISE IS A CHOICE

The Lord tells us in Deuteronomy 30:15 (NASU): "See, I have set before you today life and prosperity, and death and adversity." God has set it all out before us. The choice lies with us, and it is definitely a choice. "Oh, I choose life!" we say on Sunday morning when the preacher reads that Scripture in Deuteronomy, but Sunday morning is not when the choice is really made. It is more likely made on Monday or Wednesday, when life crashes in on us. It is then that we can either allow ourselves to be overrun with the devil's propaganda or get up and fight back in praise. If we make the choice to lie down under the enemy's barrage, our circumstances will surely get the best of us. Our passivity will determine our downfall, but if we make the choice to rise up and praise our God, He will inhabit our praises (Ps. 22:3), and we will reconnect to the "Father of lights" from whom every good thing comes down (James 1:17).

We have to command our soul to be encouraged, rise up from all oppression, and start praising!

David had to make that choice. Sometimes he just had to tell himself to praise. In Psalm 103:1, he said, "Bless the LORD, O my soul; and all that is within me, bless His holy name!" Everything within David might not have wanted to bless the Lord right at that time. He had to tell himself to do it anyway. This is a good example for us. If David didn't want to praise the Lord all the time, we don't have to feel so bad about ourselves. We do have to do what David did when he felt that way. We have to command our soul to be encouraged, rise up from all oppression, and start praising! The writer of Hebrews said, "…lift up the hands which hang down" (Heb. 12:12, KJV). That's just a choice we have to make—not just if we feel like it or if we are adequately inspired. We just need to do it. It is for our own good and well-being.

GOD ENTHRONES HIMSELF ON OUR PRAISE

In Psalm 22, Jesus speaks prophetically through David. It is the scene of the Crucifixion, one thousand years in the future. Jesus speaks the words that He would one day speak from the cross, "My God, My God, why have You forsaken Me?" (Ps. 22:1). But after Jesus decries His agony, He brings forth a revelation concerning what happens when we praise the Lord. "But You are holy, enthroned in the praises of Israel" (Ps. 22:3). This was a revelation that David had capitalized on in his tabernacle. If God establishes His throne on our praise, then imagine how beneficial it would be to maintain that praise all the time. God would be continually enthroned, and from that throne, He would be continually ruling in favor of Israel. David put over four thousand Levites to work in the tabernacle, a fresh team each hour of the day and night so that they would not get tired and become slack in their praises. Each hour a new group of Levites would enter the tabernacle to praise the Lord with all their might.

For twenty-four hours a day, David's Levites enthroned the Lord on their praises, and God, from His throne, ruled greatly on David's behalf. David's military commanders began to take a vested interest in what went on in the tabernacle while they were out on the battlefield (1 Chron. 25:1). David let the commanders help choose who would be ministering before the Lord. They knew the ones they wanted—the most vibrant, the most anointed, and the most passionate worshipers. Psalm 119:164 says, "Seven times a day I praise You." That could be a goal. We could praise the Lord when we first get up in the morning, on our ten o'clock break, at noon, on our afternoon break, at supper with the family, and again before we go to bed. But wait—that is only six times. We'll need one more time sometime during the day. However, remember that God made evening before morning. I believe that God will cause us to arise in one of the night watches. If we begin that watch with praise, we will see our entire day ordered with praise.

FROM CELEBRATION TO JUBILATION

The next step for the body of Christ is to go from praise to celebration to jubilation. What does this mean? Haven't we done enough by praising? Haven't we connected with God, changed the atmosphere, and determined the perspective? If we have done these things, then we have done a lot, but there is one more step that we must take—the *coup de grâce*. This phrase means "the blow of mercy" in French and is used to describe "a death blow intended to end the suffering of a wounded creature. It is often used figuratively to describe the last of a series of events that brings about the end of some entity."[11]

That entity for us is the devil's kingdom and his power over us. Our praise is awesome and powerful, but when we take that up a notch to celebration and then to jubilation, our sound becomes a death blow to the enemy's plans for us. I love the words *celebration* and *jubilation*. In the Bible, *celebrate* is from the Hebrew word *hagag*, which denotes a wild action like the behavior of a drunken person, used in the context of rejoicing. You know how we get sometimes when we've just won the big game—we shout, scream, jump up and down, and hug everyone (while jumping up and down). Someone could easily think we are drunk, except no one is watching each other—we are all caught up in the spirit of celebration and victory. The emotion of the moment has overtaken the atmosphere. The rapturous spirit has overcome the environment.

The word *hagag* was used to depict the dancing and rejoicing that was done when there was a victory over the enemy in battle, as in 1 Samuel 30:16 (NIV) when David came upon the Amalekites who had plundered his city of Ziklag: "There they were, scattered over the countryside, eating, drinking and *reveling* because of the great amount of plunder they had taken" (emphasis added). The word *reveling* in this passage is the Hebrew word *hagag*. The Amalekites were celebrating their victory.

Their actions were wild and appeared hedonistic. We will discuss situations like this in a later chapter. This was how David made it through every narrow transition.

When David was rebuked by his wife Michal for his dancing and celebration in the streets before the ark, David told his wife, "You ain't seen nothing yet!" (2 Sam. 6:22, author's paraphrase). This must be our attitude, because invariably there will be those who want us to tone down our celebration before the Lord to show respect for a religious kingdom that is in place. However, we must remember that the kingdom of God is ever changing. Every time glory comes into our worship in a new way, the manner in which we demonstrate and administrate the power of God changes.

Though numerous victories are still in the future, they are all as good as done in the mind of the Lord.

Jubilation, while similar in meaning to *celebration*, is the act of rejoicing, being filled, and expressing great joy. Here is what I consider a key part of the definition: "...especially because of triumph or success."[12] Just like celebration, jubilation depends on the aspect of triumph. When our favorite team or person wins, our most familiar dynamic of triumph is that we not only praise but also revel in our triumph, dancing and shouting like we just won the Super Bowl. In God there is no defeat or failing, only triumph. We must be the same about the victories of the Spirit of God in our lives. *Because of religious spirits, jubilation is the least expressed emotion of Christians.*

The Book of Revelation tells us of the final victory that we will experience. Though numerous victories are still in the future, they are all as good as done in the mind of the Lord. If we have the mind of Christ (1 Cor. 2:16), it must be the same with us. That gives us plenty to celebrate. Matt Redman tells of a time when the fervor for God inside of him just could not be discharged in the singing of the service he was in. "Becoming frantic for a way to release my worship, I hurried out of church, forgetting to put my shoes on, and ran around the parking lot for ten minutes. I must have looked like an idiot. But at the time, I couldn't have cared less. I wasn't bothered by who saw me or how weird it all looked. I was before God—and God alone....We get so caught up in love and wonder that we forget what others might think, and we throw ourselves into God's pleasure."[13]

When David put the ark in his tabernacle, he gave a charge of responsibility to the Levites. "And he appointed some of the Levites to minister before the ark of the LORD, to commemorate, to thank, and to praise the LORD God of Israel" (1 Chron. 16:4). The word that David used for praise in this passage had never been used before by the Hebrews. It is possible that the Levites asked David what the word meant, having never heard it before, although this is pure conjecture on my part. According to the Scriptures, it was a word that was used in heaven, but before David built his tabernacle, the word had never been used on Earth. (See Revelation 19:1, NIV.) The word in Hebrew was *halal*. We get our word *hallelujah* from *halal*. Although the Hebrews already had several words that David could have chosen from, God gave David a new word for praise that would be the *coup de grâce* of all the other words for praise.

Halal went beyond singing, shouting, raising the hands, and proclaiming God's mighty deeds. *Halal* means "to shine" or, more completely, to make a show of your praise with loud boasting and raving like a madman. This is not what most of us mean when we say "Hallelujah!" at church. We mean "Oh, boy!" or "That's great!" Because we are in church, we have to use our Christian lingo. When David gave the word to his Levites, he meant for them to get into such a mind-set of victory that their normal manner of praise would not be able to express it. That's the way it is in heaven. In the Book of Revelation we see a picture of worship as it is in heaven. In chapter 19 they enter into *halal*. "After these things I heard something like a loud voice of a great multitude in heaven, saying, 'Hallelujah! Salvation and glory and power belong to our God'" (Rev. 19:1, NASU, emphasis added).

The call to the heavenly worshipers to *halal* or to make a show of their praise with boasting and noisy raving is the created atmosphere of heaven. If we really believe the Lord's Prayer, "Your will be done on earth as it is in heaven," we must know that our call on Earth is to reflect the worshipers of heaven and *halal* with all of our might! Without extensive study into the original Hebrew language, you can see that our word *hallelujah* has this hidden meaning. Every time we shout *hallelujah*, we are stirring the winds of heaven in the earth realm. Paul gives us the perfect picture of our celebration in 2 Corinthians 2:14: "Now thanks be to God who always leads us in triumph in Christ."

That word *triumph* was used in Paul's day to denote the triumphal entry of celebrated Roman generals on their return from a victorious campaign of war. All of the general's spoils of war were paraded through the streets for everyone to see. The people cheered, and his soldiers sang songs of praise. Thanks be to God, who always leads us, through Christ, in a joyous triumphal entry procession! This is a time in history when the ark is in procession again. In other words, God's glory is moving back into His church in a way that our generations have not known. We must make a move now to enter into celebration and jubilation and deliver that *coup de grâce* to the enemy's schemes toward us. *Halal!*

THE KINGDOM IS ADVANCING

Blessings are surrounding you, but you must learn how to open the door so they can manifest in your sphere of influence and the territory in which you dwell. I pray that the blessings of God manifest in each one of you. Third John 2, says: "Beloved, I pray that you may prosper in all things and be in health, just as your soul prospers." In Psalms we read:

> To You I will cry, O Lord my Rock...
> Hear the voice of my supplications
> When I cry to You,
> When I lift up my hands toward Your holy sanctuary....
>
> The Lord is my strength and my shield...
> And with my song I will praise Him.

The LORD is their strength,
And He is the saving refuge [or defense] of His anointed.

—Psalm 28:1–2, 7–8

May you have confidence in prayer. May you find your place in His sanctuary and boldly enter the throne room of grace. May you be filled with renewed joy. May all the trials and discouragement of this past season and any hope deferred be gone from you. May your soul rejoice and prosper. May the work of your hands prosper. May He work in you mightily to do His will. May the gifts of God within you be released and activated. May a new anointing arise within you and favor be seen upon you. May He defend His anointed. May your shield of faith be polished and renewed.

Isaiah 41 tells us: "Fear not, for I am with you; be not dismayed, for I am your God. I will strengthen you, yes, I will help you, I will uphold you with My righteous right hand.... Those who war against you shall be as nothing.... 'Fear not, I will help you'" (Isa. 41:10, 12–13). The Lord is in the process of changing our identity. No longer will we be known as we presently are, but we will be known as kingdom people who are ready to stand against the gates of hell, submit to God, resist His enemies, and watch them flee. We are moving from just a "church" mentality to a "kingdom" mentality. In other words, we are moving from gathering and fellowship to dominion.

MOVING WITH THE KING!

A kingdom has a king. The king is the supreme head of the nation. God's people began with judges, but the more they went up against the enemies in Canaan, the more they realized that their government was different from the foes they were warring against. The king was the commander in chief of the army. He was the supreme judge and absolute master of the lives of his subjects. He exercised taxes and exacted service upon request. The king, who represented the kingdom, was set apart, consecrated, and anointed with oil. The king was also known as "the Lord's anointed." His subjects were required to represent him fully. He was responsible for the overall use of the revenue of the kingdom. He had an extensive court to operate and accomplish his wishes in representing the kingdom. He was king, and he had subjects. This was kingdom life. The king's territory had boundaries, and he had sovereign rule in the boundaries. If you did not move with the king as you were requested, then you were declared a rebel.

The Israelites seem to have been convinced that they could not succeed against their formidable enemies unless, like other nations, they placed themselves under the rule of a king. Probably another influencing cause was the disgust excited by the corrupt administration of affairs by the sons of Samuel and the desire for a radical change. (See 1 Samuel 8:3–6.) Accordingly, the original idea of a Hebrew king was twofold: first, that he should lead the people to battle in time of war, and second, that he should execute judgment and justice for them in war and peace (1 Sam. 8:20).[14]

KINGDOM OF GOD

Kingdom life in the earth realm was used to help individuals understand the kingdom of God. There are two terms throughout the Bible that we must embrace and understand: the *kingdom of God* and the *kingdom of heaven*. Anyone who willingly subjects himself to the sovereign rule of a holy God is aligned with kingdom principles. The *kingdom of heaven* represents the rule that God asserts on the earth at any given period in time. This is what links kingdom understanding to time. John the Baptist, Jesus, and the apostles all announced that the kingdom of God was "at hand." As a matter of fact, the Lord said, "The kingdom of God is within you" (Luke 17:21). If this is so, then when the king moves, we must move with Him.

According to Matthew 13:24–30, 36–43, the present gospel age represents the mystery form of the kingdom. "Since the kingdom of heaven is no other than the rule of God on the earth, He must now be ruling to the extent of full realization of those things which are termed 'the mysteries' in the New Testament and which really constitute the new message of the New Testament."[15]

The manifested rule of God on the earth is ever maturing. The fullness of this rule will not be recognized until the millennial period when Christ returns. However, the king is moving us from just going to church to understanding His kingdom in our territory. He is bringing us into a place of dominion, occupation, and rule with Him in the spheres and places to which He has assigned us. Jesus taught so much on the kingdom. The kingdom is good news! Kingdom life was proclaimed during the three years that Jesus ministered in the earth realm, for which we have a record of His mediational authority. Every time we mediate with Him, we are operating in kingdom rule. This is what makes His rule and reign occur in every generation in the earth realm.

The kingdom cannot be controlled by civil government.

The kingdom is *not* based on needs, since "the poor you have with you always" (John 12:8). Jesus gave us a responsibility to work with the poor, orphans, and widows, but on the other hand, He also showed us the necessity to lavishly worship Him as Mary did in John 10. The kingdom cannot be controlled by civil government. Through the ages, civil government has made an attempt to govern and rule God's government in the earth. However, the kingdom is not based on worldly patterns.

Another important fact that we must all recognize is that we cannot comprehend the kingdom by our natural mind. The mind is in enmity with God and longs to be conformed by the world around it. However, as we renew our mind, we break out of worldly conformity and move into seeing kingdom life in the midst of the societal structures that are molding us. The kingdom cannot be obtained by ambition. James, John, and Judas were all confronted by the Lord as they attempted to operate in worldly ambition in the midst of His kingdom plan. John and James submitted. Judas would never submit; therefore, the son of perdition entered Judas. In other words, he became a son of the dark world.

His life ended prematurely without any connection to the One who had discipled him.

The exciting thing about the kingdom is that it cannot be *postponed!* The kingdom is filled with power. Over these last two decades we have seen kingdom government for the next season of God in the earth realm. Kingdom people understand kingdom grace. The kingdom is ruled by grace and love, not by rules, regulations, and laws. God has appointed kingdom administrators for every age. We find those gifts listed in Ephesians 4:11–13:

> And He Himself gave some to be apostles, some prophets, some evangelists, and some pastors and teachers, for the equipping of the saints for the work of ministry, for the edifying of the body of Christ, till we all come to the unity of the faith and of the knowledge of the Son of God, to a perfect man, to the measure of the stature of the fullness of Christ.

Every kingdom has a culture. We must represent the culture of the kingdom that we are aligned with. God's kingdom is filled with His glory. We are moving from glory to glory. You are being positioned to make a transition into the next realm of glory.

CHAPTER 6

A TIME TO BE POSITIONED FOR YOUR FUTURE

I N 1 CORINTHIANS 10:11 PAUL MAKES A STATEMENT IN CONNECtion with the Book of Numbers. This admonition brings clarity to our future. Chuck Missler says the following about this connection: "Why does the Bible record all the things that happened during those forty years? The Scripture tells us it was for an example. These things happened to them for our admonition. Paul makes a point in 1 Corinthians 10:11 that everything written then is for our application now. Every one of the events in Numbers has a lesson for us. That's why it is so important to study this book in detail. The word *example* in Greek is *tupos*, which is 'a figure, an image, a pattern, a pre-figuring.' That's where we get the term *type* or *model*. Engineers speak of a prototype, which is from the same root. Types are common in the Bible, where some event, some object, or some situation is a lesson, in advance, of what's coming. The manna we read about in the Book of Numbers is a type, as is the brazen serpent and the water from the rock."[1]

A VIOLENT, OVERCOMING, PRAISING, CORPORATE REMNANT IS ARISING

To be positioned for our future properly, we must look at past models and examples that occurred in different generations in different historical settings. Matthew 11:12 says, "And from the days of John the Baptist until *now* the kingdom of heaven suffers violence, *and the violent take it by force*" (emphasis added). Therefore, the violence through the ages in God's kingdom is very applicable and brings much-needed wisdom to us as we move forward today. We can actually trace "kingdom violence" from the time of John the Baptist until now.

This scripture has always intrigued me. *Violence* is an interesting word to use in relationship to God's kingdom plan. After growing up in the midst of domestic violence for years, *violent* was not a word with which I could associate the kingdom of God. From a negative connotation, violence is the violation of God's perfect order. In the midst of this violation, instability in our life is produced. I will discuss this in my next book on time, *Redeeming the Times: Unlocking Your God Potential for Success!*

However, when meditating on the above scripture, which declares that the kingdom of heaven is taken by the force of the *violent* (a noun form referring to a people), I had to seek the Lord for the positive slant on this very physical word! When God is talking about us being violent, I have sensed that He needs to describe us in this manner. A violent people taking the kingdom by force is a people that He is raising up who will press through difficult, stormy situations filled with persecutions and force an atmospheric change. This is a revolutionary group of individuals who will not be content until they see a manifestation of God's kingdom in the earth. Faith will be our victory.

Force is a word that denotes power, strength, and straining. Here are ten issues that will better explain the concept that Jesus was attempting to bring forth through the ages.

1. *He will have a people filled with strength.* This violent group of people will have active and vigorous power. They will demonstrate might and produce action against forces that are counteracting their goals.

2. *He will have a people who gain momentum.* As this people go against their enemy, their actions will increase in motion. In other words, the more they move, the more they will keep moving. Albert Einstein once said, "Life is like riding a bicycle. To keep your balance you must keep moving."[2]

3. *He will have a people of accurate moral reason and judgment.* Their minds and wills are to be empowered by His understanding. They will be a people who know how to argue heaven's cause in the earth.

4. *He will have a people of violence.* They will exert compulsory power against resisting forces and conquer that which intends to stop their forward movement.

5. *He will have a people of virtue.* The Proverbs 31 woman is a great example of a violent person who causes her household to prosper. This woman had power to produce effects in converting resources.

6. *He will have a people who have the power to bind and loose.* They will be able to look at contracts and declare them either valid or invalid.

7. *He will have a people of destiny.* They will use divine decrees to open up the way to accomplish every mission to which they are assigned.

8. *He will have a people who move like a raging storm in the earth.* When a territory or region has been violated through iniquity, they will create a storm of change to restore that territory back to God's original plan of fullness.

9. *He will have a people who, like Jesus, fulfill the law without being confined by the law of the earth.* They will remain within the boundaries that have been set but will reset boundaries that have been violated.

10. *He will have a people filled with strength and power for war.* A violent people is like a troop who drives out an enemy force and establishes a beachhead for future victory.

FORCE AND TIME

An object with momentum is going to be hard to stop. To stop such an object, it is necessary to apply a force against its motion for a given period of time. The more momentum an object has, the harder it is to stop. Thus, it would require a greater amount of force or a longer amount of time (or both) to bring an object with more momentum to a halt. As the force acts upon the object for a given amount of time, the object's velocity is changed; and hence, the object's momentum is changed.... An object with momentum can be stopped if a force is applied against it for a given amount of time. A force acting for a given amount of time will change an object's momentum. Put another way, an unbalanced force always accelerates an object—either speeding it up or slowing it down. If the force acts opposite the object's motion, it slows the object down. If a force acts in the same direction as the object's motion, then the force speeds the object up. Either way, a force will change the velocity of an object. And if the velocity of the object is changed, then the momentum of the object is changed.... Force multiplied by time equals the mass multiplied by the change in velocity. In physics, the quantity Force*time is known as the impulse.[3]

There are several ways in which most of us can relate to this principle. The first way I learned the concept of impulse came when I was learning to ride a horse. I was unable to control the power of the horse, and the horse, instead of me and the bridle, began to direct our path. As the horse's momentum continued to increase, I found myself hanging on with no ability to direct the power or produce an action. Our path led us under my grandmother's clothesline. The horse's momentum continued, but I ended up stopped by the clothesline.

Most of us understand this concept of momentum from driving an automobile. When I was learning to drive, which I did at a very young age, I had to learn some hard lessons. By understanding the above principle, we know that there is an amount of time between applying a car's brakes and the actual moment when the car stops. The first vehicle I drove was a five-speed stick-shift truck. I got going and kept going until one of the telephone poles that was used for our horse training arena stopped me. I had to learn the power ratio of vehicle to man. I still have a very healthy respect for a car's power.

Impulse is force being communicated. Impulse involves one body, individual, or kingdom working against another. Impulse is the effect of motion. Once things get in motion, they are hard to stop. The body of Christ is advancing. The kingdom is advancing. The violent are taking the kingdom of heaven by force. There are certain changes creating motion that cannot be stopped. The kingdom of darkness must give way to the kingdom of God, which is advancing with new strength. The supernatural power of God being released on His people is creating much motion and change in the earth. We are under the impulsion or driving force of a King who wants to see change in the world today. As we learn to move in our proper spheres of authority in the earth realm, we will harness God's power, and when we release that power, transformation will occur in cities and nations.

A TIME TO MOVE FROM FELLOWSHIP TO WAR

The Lord is moving in a new way in today's church. The move of God is accelerating. God's people are gaining a new strength and power, and they are becoming a force to be contended with in the world. After four hundred years, God's perfect time came to bring the children of Israel out of Egypt. Exodus 6:26 says that He brought them out by "armies." In war, there is an order and sound that lead God's people into victory. With the Israelites, the order of battle was simple. The force was drawn up, either in a line or in three divisions with a center and two wings. There was a rear guard to provide protection on the march or to bring in stragglers. (See Numbers

> *The kingdom of darkness must give way to the kingdom of God, which is advancing with new strength.*

10:25; Joshua 6:9; Judges 7:16; 1 Samuel 11:11; Isaiah 58:8.) The signal for the charge and the retreat was given by the sound of a trumpet. There was a battle cry to inspire courage and to impart confidence. (See Judges 7:20; Amos 1:14.)

We must have a clear trumpet sound and release of revelation at this time in history. Jesus said that He would build His church on revelation. He also said He would give us the keys to the kingdom and the gates of hell would not prevail against us. This prophetic word that He gave to Peter is still working in His people today. The Spirit of God has a goal for us. That goal is for us to occupy or take possession of the portion or sphere of authority that we each have been allotted. How we steward the possessions that God has given us is critical to our future. We must remember that when God promised Abraham a land, within that promise were included all the enemies of that land. Therefore, many times in order to take possession of something, we must first go to war. We must learn to follow our king into battle and establish His dominion within each one of our assignments.

The church is moving from fellowship to war. *Church*, which means "gathering," has been known as a place to socialize and meet the needs of the members involved in each gathering. I don't want to say that we will not continue to do this, but I do believe that we are gaining momentum as we move toward being a revolutionary, transformational organism in the earth. To bring great change into society, we must be a people of strategy. *Strategy* is a war word.

I have written several books related to warfare. I would not want to take the space in this book to communicate all the principles of war. However, here are a few important examples of how we are making a shift now in the body of Christ:

1. *We must go forward only with the Lord's marching orders.* Joshua 6–7 are great examples for us as we go forth to possess our inheritance. The Israelites moved from a very strategic plan that enabled them to overcome the greatest stronghold to defeat and discouragement in the Promised

Land. This occurs when we move forward without gaining marching orders first.

2. *We must know who our captains are and who is leading us into our battles ahead.* (See Deuteronomy 20.) Leadership is very important in winning any battle. In the Old Testament, God had captains. In the New Testament, He has apostles and prophets.

3. *We must learn to defy the enemy's voice.* The story of David and Goliath is one of the most famous stories in the Bible. When David happened upon the battlefield, he was unable to listen to the voice of the Philistine's main communicator, Goliath, who had been taunting the armies of God for forty straight days. Goliath had filled the atmosphere with unbelief. David defied his voice and eventually overtook his headship.

4. *We must seek God to gain His prophetic strategy.* When Jehoshaphat was confronted with a confederation of enemies who were set on overcoming God's plan for Judah, he did not succumb to fear. Rather, he sought the Lord, fasted, and then listened to the voice of the prophet who gave him a strategy for advancement. He later said that if we will listen to the prophets, we will prosper. This statement was made before he went into battle, and he eventually gathered the spoils of war for three days.

5. *We must learn to overcome scattering and hope deferred.* The best picture of this is in the prophetic story of the dry bones in Ezekiel 37. Rebecca Wagner Sytsema and I write about this in *God's Now Time for Your Life.*[4] We give a detailed account of how there are four levels of prophetic decrees that are necessary to break the power of scattering in our life and bring us back to a place of fulfilling our

destiny. Our warfare is usually with the hope deferred that we have experienced from loss in our past.

6. *We must first bind the strongman.* Any time Jesus gives a first principle, that principle must be followed. He told us in Matthew 12 that if we were going to take the spoils of the enemy, we would have to first bind the strongman who was holding our spoils in captivity.

7. *We must be dressed properly to go to war.* I suggest you read both Psalm 18 and Ephesians 6. God has given us an armor that is capable of quenching every one of the enemy's fiery darts.

8. *We must learn to give our way into our promise.* Not only was this Father's plan for our redemption (John 3:16), but we also find that Abraham used this same principle in his quest to enter God's covenant plan in the earth. He gave it to Melchizedek after he warred and defeated the five kings in Genesis 14. He presented the spoils of war as an offering to someone more legitimate than himself. Our giving is a tremendous warfare tool.

9. *We must learn to find our position in God's corporate warfare plan.* We are a corporate people even though we operate very independently in the earth. This, perhaps, will produce the greatest change that the body of Christ has known. When you read Revelation 19 you find the King of kings and Lord of lords leading His troops to overthrow the beast and his army.

10. *We must know when the dragon is at our door.* Revelation 12 is probably one of the most important passages of Scripture for us to understand at this hour in history. In the midst of birthing the next reformation move of God, we must learn to protect the "Child" from the "dragon."

Hell Has a Strategy

We must always remember the prophetic word God gave Peter in Matthew 16:18: "And the gates of Hades [hell] shall not prevail" against those who have the keys of the kingdom. However, that does not mean that Satan and his government of darkness will not devise a plan to overcome God's people. But the kingdom moving with the momentum of God backing it will overcome because "He who is in you is greater than he who is in the world" (1 John 4:4)!

However, we must be aware of the dark kingdom's strategies. Satan will devise a strategy of unbelief to make your spirit numb. He will attempt to set up betrayal situations in your life to overwhelm you. He will use rejection and abandonment to make you feel fatherless and hopeless. He will take the iniquitous patterns that have hindered your bloodline and attempt to hold you captive today. He will try to keep the cycles of iniquity working from generation to generation. He will use your times of vulnerability to develop a strategy of loss and poverty in your life. He will set strongholds in place in your life so he can plunder your life year after year. He will attempt to distract you so you never harvest your field. He will make you think that God is holding out on you and entice your desires to take what is forbidden. The enemy will compete with God's voice to usurp His destiny in your life.

God Has a Passover Time

But God...! He has a time of deliverance planned for each of us so we can choose to move from a path of destruction to a path of redemption. There is a *Passover time* for your life. There has already been a sacrifice made for your freedom. From the time man sinned, the Lord had a plan of freedom. The blood is life.

> It was symbolic for the present time in which both gifts and sacrifices are offered which cannot make him who performed the service perfect in regard to the conscience—concerned only with foods and drinks, various washings, and fleshly ordinances imposed until the

143

time of reformation. But Christ came as High Priest of the good things to come, with the greater and more perfect tabernacle not made with hands, that is, not of this creation. Not with the blood of goats and calves, but with His own blood He entered the Most Holy Place once for all, having obtained eternal redemption. For if the blood of bulls and goats and the ashes of a heifer, sprinkling the unclean, sanctifies for the purifying of the flesh, how much more shall the blood of Christ, who through the eternal Spirit offered Himself without spot to God, cleanse your conscience from dead works to serve the living God?

—HEBREWS 9:9–14

As the blood circulates through our body, we experience life. This is the fluid God chose to place within us that would produce unity in the soul (Gen. 9:4). All activity of the body is dependent on the quantity of the blood that is flowing through us. The Lord knew that without the shedding of blood there could be no forgiveness. True sacrifice is linked with blood. Hebrews 9:22 says, "And according to the law almost all things are purified with blood, and without shedding of blood there is no remission." In man, God created a conscience that could be liberated by His Spirit moving through our blood system to cleanse us and create freedom in us.

Passover is an event! Each one of us must have a Passover time in our life when the power of death and captivity is broken and we move toward our promised destiny! Passover was a time of confrontation when the Lord revealed His power. This time of confrontation resulted in natural laws being invaded with divine supernatural activity. The final confrontation came when the *blood* became the way into freedom. This is an example for us today.

Without the shedding of blood there could be no forgiveness.

144

PASSOVER REPRESENTS THE DEPARTURE OUT OF CAPTIVITY

All revelation is timed. "On this rock I will build My church," says the Lord (Matt. 16:18). That rock is revelation released from Father in heaven that allows His will to be activated in the earth realm. Biblically, revelation is timed and built around three feast times: Passover, Pentecost, and the Feast of Tabernacles. These three feasts represent three cycles in each human's life. These are phases that we each must go through.

The word *captivity* refers to one being taken as a spoil of an enemy! There is a shout in each of us that must be decreed. That shout is, "I am coming out and crossing over into my inheritance!" After rereading the story of the children of Israel and their arrival in Israel, the Lord quickened to me the following issues concerning captivity. *Captivity* can also mean one confined to his or her present place. The place might be good, but not God's best! If you are experiencing any captivity or wish to be enlarged, consider the following:

1. How was your captivity initiated? Joseph shared his dream out of season and ended up in captivity.

2. Did God initiate your captivity, or did you do something to cause this? Remember, Joseph's brothers were remorseful for allowing Joseph to end up in captivity. Joseph said later, "You meant evil against me; but God meant it for good" (Gen. 50:20). Therefore, your captivity can always turn to good.

3. Remember that seventy people left Canaan, their Promised Land, and went into Egypt. There they prospered, and the Egyptian king proclaimed, "Look, the people of the children of Israel are more and mightier than we" (Exod. 1:9). You can prosper in your captivity. However, your prosperity is not always your place of promise.

4. Look for change in authority structures. "There arose a new king over Egypt, who did not know Joseph" (Exod. 1:8). Changes in authority are key signs for us to watch closely so that we can see our window of opportunity.

5. The Egyptian midwives were ordered to kill the Hebrew children (Exod. 1:15–16). However, they refused. Know that there are advocates on your path who will represent God's purpose to protect you.

6. Jochebed (Moses's mother) used resources that she had to protect Moses. While you are in captivity the Lord can show you how to use resources that will sustain you until you can move into your future.

7. God is always preparing a deliverer. Moses was there at the right time.

8. Do not be afraid to confront the enemy. Moses did not know what he was doing when he entered into this supernatural realm. He took what he had (his rod) and began to use it to break an entire nation out of captivity. Just take what you have and let the Spirit of God breathe on it, and begin to move supernaturally in a new way.

COMING FULL CIRCLE, BEING RELEASED FROM YOUR WILDERNESS, AND MOVING TOWARD YOUR PROMISE

Israel first had to complete the four hundred years that were decreed by the Lord for the Israelites' captivity in Egypt. Sometimes we are destined to wait until God's perfect time of release. However, I do not believe it was God's perfect plan for them to wander in the wilderness. Even in wandering, there is a perfect time of release. As we said at the beginning of this chapter, we can learn from past mistakes and from the people who represent the same covenant into which we are grafted.

When we miss one opportunity, the Lord brings us full circle to offer us the best again. We do not want to repeat our wanderings and go through the same cycle again. Moses recorded these wanderings in Numbers 33. He takes thirty-six verses to cover about thirty-eight years. Deuteronomy 2:14 says that the time it took to go from Kadesh Barnea back to the plains of Moab, until the older generation died, was thirty-eight years. We have already discussed the man at the Pool of Bethesda in an earlier chapter. He had been held in his infirmity for thirty-eight years. Old cycles can hang on for years, even generations. Satan loves to keep these cycles in operation from generation to generation in our lives.

> *Now is the time to break from any old cycle that has held your promise and destiny in captivity.*

BE SURE *OLD CYCLES* ARE BROKEN

Israel was an example of a corporate group who had to overcome several things to enter the Promised Land. The following spiritual assignment will allow us to move forward into the fullness of God's plan for our lives. Before you read further, *make a list of old cycles.* Now is the time to break from any old cycle that has held your promise and destiny in captivity. Declare that your Passover time of deliverance is now beginning. Ask God for signs, wonders, and miracles that will intervene in old cyclical structures of your life. Be secure in timing. Declare that everything in your past be repaired and restored so that your future can be unlocked. Look up and see the window of heaven that is opening over you. Gain victory in strategic warfare. Do not be afraid to ascend in worship. This is a time to experience God's glory. Draw near to God, and He will draw near to you. Ask God to open your eyes so you can see His glory. *Make a list of promises.* Even *make a list of stirrings that have been in your heart that have never come to fullness.* Let His presence direct you into the path of deliverance and *Passover* from captivity to freedom. Position yourself for your future. The best is ahead!

POSITIONED BY HIS PRESENCE

To understand our future, we need to look at certain principles that have been communicated to us by a holy God from heaven and patterns of victory that have been established as examples from the past. *Future* is such an interesting concept and dimension to meditate on. I discussed the whole premise of the word *future* in chapter 2. You may return there for a review of how *future* relates to expectations and creates either fear and anxiety or hope and faith in us. Let's now look at the principle of being positioned for the future. How does our positioning set our course for the days ahead? Why was God so interested in our positioning or place? Again, Acts 17:26 says that He has predetermined our time and our boundaries!

Biblically, *presence* is associated with *face*. Will we look into His face to gain the reflection we need to advance? For man to advance, he must communicate with his maker. We must overcome all veiled structures and blocked communication lines and receive God's will in heaven and perform that will in the earth. All men and women should have the same goal as Abraham—to become a friend of God and daily be in communion with Him. God has always been known to manifest His presence through visitation. He does this sometimes through dreams and visions so we can enter into His plan of fullness for our lives. He can send angels or even cause a "bush to burn" that will initiate our turning aside to be encountered by Him. We can still be like Moses and know Him face-to-face.

TRUMPETS AND CLOUDS

His presence not only positions us for our future but also guides us on a daily basis. His presence keeps us in His perfect timing. We discussed trumpets in relationship to praise and sound in the last chapter, but let's now look at trumpets in relationship to movement. In God's kingdom, movement and advancement should always be linked with presence.

When the cloud starts moving and the trumpet starts blowing, the body of Christ must move forward, accelerate, and keep going.

We find in Numbers 9 that throughout the Israelites' journey in the wilderness, the Lord accompanied them by means of the miraculous cloud of glory, which overshadowed the camp. When the cloud lifted, indicating the time for breaking camp had arrived, the priesthood sounded a long trumpet blast on a pair of silver trumpets to alert the people that the time for setting out had arrived. They also used other distinctive trumpet blasts. They sounded staccato trumpet blasts to convene the assembly. The priests sounded different combinations of trumpet blasts for declaring the onset of festivals and Sabbaths and other blasts for invoking divine assistance in battle.

The use of the trumpets to indicate the onset of the Sabbath and appointed times carried over into temple practice and, even later, into synagogue practice. Rabbis taught the following:

> Six blasts were blown on Friday evening before the Sabbath. The first one warned people to cease working in the fields. The second one warned people in the city to cease working. The third warned people to kindle their Sabbath lights.... [finally the last three] a *tekiah*, *teruah*, and a *tekiah* were blown to mark the onset of the Sabbath....
>
> Jerusalem archaeology has revealed a stone, part of the second temple from the days of the apostles, on which the words, "to the place of the trumpeting for" are inscribed. Archaeologists surmise that the stone might have originally read, "To the place of the trumpeting for the priests." It must have once marked the station high up on the temple pinnacle where the priests stood to blast the trumpets at the beginning of Sabbaths and festivals.[5]

Therefore, we can surmise that sound and presence work together from heaven into the earth to guide us forward and keep us timed in decisions, confrontations, and victories in the earth. Sound and presence always accompany visitation and will continue until the Lord's final return. There is that appointed time when all of Israel calls on the

Lord and the great cloud of faithful witnesses assemble for their rule. Daniel describes our Lord as: "One like a Son of Man, coming with the clouds of heaven" (Dan. 7:13).

The Placement of the Tabernacle in the Midst of the Tribes

The presence of God was positioned at the center of the Israelites' community life. In the garden, it was God's intent for the communion and our devotional life to be the center of all activities. His presence walked and talked with man and woman as they worked. As they worked, they worshiped. This pattern now must be restored from generation to generation so God's intent for the earth and mankind can continue.

How the physical community was positioned and established expressed the spiritual life of the community. God truly stood at the center of a community with the expressed goal of the community reflecting His image in all of their activities. The way He positioned the twelve tribes was an ideal prototype of God's relationship with man in any community. Israel was compared to a vine. In Numbers 2:2, God speaks to Moses and Aaron declaring, "Everyone of the children of Israel shall camp by his own standard, beside the emblems of his father's house; they shall camp some distance from the tabernacle of meeting." God does not whimsically or haphazardly plant His vine. Israel was arranged under separate standards—each tribe by its own standard, according to the tribe's emblems.

Numbers 3:38, says, "Moreover those who were to camp before the tabernacle on the east, before the tabernacle of meeting, were Moses, Aaron, and his sons." Next to Moses and Aaron was the standard associated with the camp of Judah. Next to Judah's standard were the standards of Issachar and Zebulun. The Israelites always looked to the "center" for guidance. They associated with each other so they had inspiration and revelation on how to win their battles. Judah, Issachar, and Zebulun learned from the leadership of Moses, the meekest man on the earth. Because Moses had encountered God face-to-face and received His call from the burning bush, he could disciple Judah, Issachar, and Zebulun, who had been held captive in Egypt.

While the tabernacle stood in the center, the tribes encamped around the periphery: Asher, Dan, and Naphtali in the north; Issachar, Judah, and Zebulun in the east; Gad, Reuben, and Simeon in the south; and Benjamin, Ephraim, and Manasseh in the west. In the Promised Land the tribes were established around Jerusalem. God positioned them not only in their movement but also in their allotment in the land. In the Promised Land they were positioned from north to south in this order: Dan, Asher, Naphtali, Manasseh, Ephraim, Reuben, Judah, Jerusalem, Benjamin, Simeon, Issachar, Zebulun, and Gad.

Why the need for such placement and order? First of all, each tribe had a gift and prophetic destiny, but the fullness of their destiny depended upon the destiny of the whole. Each had weaknesses, and each had strengths. Therefore, their positioning helped in their protection and advancement as they walked together. This is just like us today. If we are positioned correctly, we can help each other accomplish our ultimate purpose in God. God has made and positioned us so we will not be able to occupy and possess what is allotted to us without moving right relationally.

> *If we are positioned correctly, we can help each other accomplish our ultimate purpose in God.*

The tribe's positioning was directly related to their movement. In Numbers 10 we find that Judah moved first. It is the same with us. We do not need to move without *praise* going before us. Judah also was a tribe of *war*. Praise and war go together. Issachar was next. Issachar stands for *timing, intercession,* and *wages.* Next was Zebulun, which means *a good dowry.* You want the dowry to accomplish what you need to do. Reuben, Simeon, and Gad moved next. As you see the redemptive qualities of the tribes and their order, you can understand the movement going around you. Next were Ephraim, Manasseh, and Benjamin. Last were Dan, Asher, and Naphtali. If you are moving right, then signs, wonders, and riches will follow you.

The tabernacle was centered by God in the midst of the tribes so the Israelites would never forget that God should always be the center of their worship and movement. Recognizing God's presence and His mobility was key to Israel's advancement and victories. The same recognition is necessary for us today. We must not journey without Him. The pillar of cloud and fire symbolized His presence. These two manifestations would rise from the tabernacle as a signal that the time had come to move forward toward the Promised Land.

Not until the Israelites were to cross the Jordan into Canaan did this forty-year phenomenon end. However, to go into Canaan, God changed the way the people were to view His presence. Now instead of the cloud and fire, the ark of the covenant of God would go before them and lead them into conquest of their promise (Josh. 3:1–4). The ark was the driving force until the time of Eli when the people lost their awe of God's presence and the ark went into Philistine captivity (1 Sam. 4:3–11). If we do not honor His presence and revere and fear Him, captivity is our ultimate destiny. God has never limited Himself in how He manifests. Throughout history He has continued to manifest Himself in various ways. He brought down fire in Elijah's day. He also sent a gentle whisper during that time, releasing future revelation. He filled the temple in Solomon's day. He sent tongues of fire and wind during the time of the disciples. He has continued in history to manifest Himself. To advance, we must always recognize and embrace His presence.

GATHER TOGETHER TO
HEAR YOUR FUTURE

I have meditated on the movement and positioning of the tribes for several years. Let me attempt to communicate the prophetic significance of this revelation. We must not look at God's revelation from an earthly human perspective and fail to embrace how He is moving and working in us today. Let's first look at Jacob.

Genesis 25:26 says, "Afterward his brother came out, and his *hand took hold* of Esau's *heel*; so his name was called Jacob. Isaac was sixty years old when she bore them" (emphasis added). Abraham, Isaac, and then Jacob were God's order for His covenant fulfillment. God knew that these three men of faith were to be prototypes for our future! All of us who would trust in Jehovah God and embrace His Son, Jesus, would have to look at the lives of these three and learn the will and workings of God so we could grasp our future. We must study their failures and victories and learn how struggles of faith are causing us to become the overcoming remnant of the future.

Have you ever had a child who was not perfect? We love to think that our children's behavior and actions would cause the world to view us as the perfect model parents. I think that is why God chose Jacob. He was the model of imperfection, marked by multiple shortcomings, manipulations, and revived vision after severe loss. He was not a perfect child, but yet he was a model and example that most of us can relate to. God was still a perfect parent of the covenant even though Jacob was a struggler. The verbal root of his name is *aqov*, which means "to restrain, to hold back or delay." It is translated in our Bibles as "heel, supplant, stay, wait, footsteps, and deceitful." The contextual use of these words is based upon our verbal root of holding something back.

We must never forget that our sons and daughters are meant to prophesy. In Genesis 49:1–2 we find a key scripture that says, "And Jacob called his sons and said, 'Gather together, that I may tell you what shall befall you in the last days: Gather together and hear, you sons of Jacob, and listen to Israel your father.'" Jacob was saying, "Let's come together so I can share your future with you. Let me prophesy to each one of you. Let me share your ensnarements and strengths, which are key for you to understand your path ahead." Therefore, from the tribes, we can understand the purpose of wholeness, interacting with each other, and how prophesy is connected with our future. Because we serve the God of Abraham, Isaac, and Jacob and through His Son have been grafted into their blessings, we need to understand the reasoning of how our latter-day revelations and victories are linked with our positioning and movement.

Developing Our Identity and Wholeness for the Future

How do we develop our identity and wholeness? First, you must understand how inheritance is developed. In studying the tribes, you develop the concept of building an overall whole identity. Once you've built the whole identity, you understand that within the whole, you have an inheritance—you have a portion. The concept of inheritance becomes very important as we move forward into understanding the tribes. *Inheritance* means "my portion." Your portion is linked with a promise. You also need to know how covenant is established. *Covenant* is an agreement in the midst of a relationship. *Established* means that your framework is established.

Another thing you want to learn is how parts are linked with the whole. That is why it is important to learn how the tribes were formed. In your life you may find that you have fragmentation in some areas, but God wants you to be whole. He doesn't want any fragmentation working independently of the whole. You can see that occur in the history of the tribes, but that was not God's ultimate plan. The whole concept of the tribes is this: even though there were tribes, God's full covenant plan was to work through the whole. Prophetic destiny is fulfilled as you find your position functionally and territorially. This is the same concept of tribe. Each of us has a prophetic destiny, a position, and a time for breakthrough.

You war from your prophetic destiny. The tribes could not go to war without the presence of God. If they went to war without the presence of God, they faltered. You find that no matter what or how you are advancing, you must learn how to operate in the presence of God in order for you to bring down what God has for you and see it manifest.

You come into the fulfillment of your inheritance through relational agreement with the Lord, and your future is dependent upon His presence. By studying the tribes, you can see prophetic fulfillment taking place. The Book of Revelation brings us into a new place of understanding the final wars linked with God's fulfilled destiny in the earth. The Book of Revelation also shows us our corporateness in that war ahead. The whole concept of the tribes was sustaining God's covenant plan from one generation to the next. God will intervene in the midst of time to see His people arise and His plans fulfilled

In our Greek culture and mind-set, we could miss the purpose of God in time. We must have a Hebraic mind-set that operates from a covenant perspective. When we think about our spiritual life from a Hebraic concept, we study from a historical perspective. So events and interactions are capsulated in a time frame. The Greek mind-set sees everything in space—concrete—and not from a time standpoint. By embracing the examples of our past,

> *When we grow up in a culture that thinks in this manner, we want everything in order, but that is not the way God works.*

we enter into a spiritual dynamic and relational dynamic with God in our time. The concrete structure of the cosmos we live in loses its blueprint of control, and we anticipate God's intervention and acceleration.

MAY GOD INTERVENE IN YOUR LIFE AND TIME TODAY

To think that the Creator of the universe has come down to the earth realm in history is mind-boggling, but to think that He will still invade and intervene in our time with revelation is mind-blowing! How overwhelming that He can connect with us, bring life to us, and activate heaven's best for us.

Because we have Greek mind-sets, we want everything to be methodized so we can get a handle on it. Method is linked with space. When we grow up in a culture that thinks in this manner, we want everything in order, but that is not the way God works. He can intervene and remove all method that we are able to grasp. That is why it is difficult for us to get in touch with God.

God is not just the God of principles. Today in many churches we teach principles, abstracts, and rules. He is not the God of abstracts;

He is the God of Abraham, Isaac, and Jacob. That is what makes God different. He decides that He is going to interact with us not based on principles but as a person whom He knit together in our mother's womb. That is what makes God so difficult to understand for so many; they do not know how to develop relationship.

He develops relationship with us by intervening, and His intervention is passed on to another person and on to another person and on to thousands of other people who came from that person. You have to come to that place of understanding what God was doing with the tribes. You can't just think substance. There is a day when God chose to intervene in someone's life to produce a tribe—whether it was Jacob with Leah, Rachel, Zilpah, or Bilhah, or Joseph with the daughter of the priest of On—God had to intervene. If you don't understand this, you miss the whole concept of God interacting with us. You miss the whole concept of covenant. Covenant is an intervention between God and mankind where they have an agreement. *Lord, don't let us miss our chosen days!* If you miss your chosen days, you will miss the movement of your tribe.

In the next chapter, we will look specifically at the tribe of Issachar, the tribe that understood time and knew what Israel should do. We must be able to hear God say, "Here is what you should do." God is intervening in our lives on a different basis every hour, every day. That is what makes Him God and what makes you so unique. You are peculiar because God intervenes with you the way you are. The God of heaven intervenes with each one, and we need to see how He is intervening with each one. That is how we see aspects of His character that we could not see any other way.

The tribe concept assures us that God has developed a model and grafted us into this model to bring us into His plan of fullness. God intervened in the days of Noah, and once again we will experience Him intervening as in the days of Noah. The name *Noah* means grace. The Lord gave him a unique plan for building and told him to build a boat when there was no rain and no plans for boats. That is who God is, and we need to understand who He is. Don't keep bringing God down to a human level. Remember that He can intervene today and tell someone something that could save us all in the future. That's who God is. Genesis 11 says that God came down to see what they were building. He did not like it, so He scattered mankind. He intervened. He is going to intervene because He made us. He has not changed. He is the same forever. We did not evolve out of nature. God intervened in the earth realm, and He formed relationship with us so we would rule nature.

If you develop this concept of God, you will develop a thinking process that will show you that you are very unique. God has created you uniquely so He can intervene with you, dialogue with you, commune with you, talk with you, and personally visit with you so that you become part of what He is doing with those with whom He has connected you. After He scattered mankind, He began to search for relationship. God has not changed. He is still looking for relationship. Abraham responded. Remember that the Lord found Abraham in Ur of Chaldea, one of the most godless places on Earth at that time. He intervened with Abraham, and Abraham responded to Him. When God intervenes with man, we must respond. If we don't, then we are going to struggle. Our emotions are going to struggle, our ways of thinking are going to struggle, and what we want to do is going to struggle. Our finances will really struggle. Abraham was prosperous in Ur, but he began to move in a new dynamic with the Lord that made him the most prosperous man on the earth. If he had not responded, God would have needed to find someone else to create the tribes, but Abraham did respond, and God blessed him. God wants us to make the effort to respond to Him so He can touch and bless us in a new way.

We must believe in who He made us to be, embrace that identity, and expect Him to intervene with us.

God believes in you. He knows you can fulfill your destiny. He believes it so much that He knit you together in your mother's womb. He finds the chosen days to intervene in our lives so we can fulfill the destiny He created us for. We must believe in who He made us to be, embrace that identity, and expect Him to intervene with us.

Revelation comes in a moment in time. How you commit to revelation is how the power and force of what was revealed manifest. Commit to His intervention when God intervenes in your life. Revelation is coming out of heaven in a moment in time. He has chosen days to reveal Himself. He chose to reveal Himself in the earth through His Son in a way we had never seen before. He will choose to reveal Himself to you in an unusual way. Know He has predetermined your times and boundaries. Ask Him to come and commune with you today.

CHAPTER 7

THROUGH TO THE NEW:
TRAVAIL, ORDER, AND TIME

I N THE LAST CHAPTER WE SAW JESUS CHANGING THE MENTALITY of the day by speaking the word in Matthew 11:12: "And from the days of John the Baptist until now the kingdom of heaven suffers violence, and the violent take it by force." He was saying to the disciples and to those listening, "The days of John are now changing; we are coming into a kingdom season in the earth. No longer are we paving the way for the kingdom. The kingdom is here!" It's the same today. We are in a season in the history of the church in which we are moving from one realm of the prophetic into another. We are moving from the "sons of thunder" realm into the "sons of Issachar" realm. In other words, we are moving past just prophesying about judgment to releasing key timing so that we as God's people will know what actions to take. We are moving into a season in which the anointing within is the most important element to get us through the narrow places on our path. This will allow us to know what God has planned and what we ought to do. In doing that, the prophetic office and gift are changing in the church, and we are moving from judgment into righteous decrees.

We are learning to discern God's perfect timing. God has us in a creative, remolding mode of development. This is a season of discipline, so we are prepared for what is ahead. This is a season of grace. In our process of learning, we are making mistakes by getting ahead or lagging behind God's timing. Every season has a beginning and an end. However, how we make it through the transitions from one season to another is the key to our future.

We have been living in a war season. War will continue to intensify in the earth realm. I believe we need a new anointing to break open God's full purposes at this time. At each breaking day of a new season, we need to have a renewed commitment to the One who made us and gives us life. Psalm 37:5–6 says, "Commit everything you do to the Lord. Trust him to help you do it, and he will. Your innocence will be clear to everyone. He will vindicate you with the blazing light of justice shining down as from the noonday sun" (TLB).

RECEIVE THE NEW

The goal we should have in each of our transitions of life is to make it from the ending of one season to the beginning of the next *new* season. The word *new* can mean something that has never been or existed before. However, new is usually defined as "different from one of the same which existed before, something stale that has been made fresh, or something of one quality that has advanced into a better quality."

Matthew 9:16 is a great example of Jesus teaching about the new. He addressed John's disciples and the Pharisees by using an analogy of a wineskin. These two groups were the two spiritual wineskins. These old skins were accusing Him over why His disciples were not having to fast the way they had fasted in the past. Jesus essentially said, "We are not going to do it the old way with the same old methods that have worked in the past!" He then said, "You cannot put new wine in an old wineskin!" (See Matthew 9:17.) In other words, there needed to be a better quality skin developed to receive what was going to be poured out in those three years when He was present with His disciples. He said, and I paraphrase, "If the new goes in the old, you will lose the old and the new. Let's preserve what has gotten us to this point. However, let's develop a new quality structure to hold the revelation that will be the fuel for us to advance."

He then moved His disciples into another teaching mode. His next assignment was to raise a twelve-year-old girl from the dead. While moving forward, a woman who had been ill with an issue of blood for twelve years pressed through the crowd to touch Him. He released His virtue, and she was immediately healed. What did this scenario represent? First of all, look at the twelve years. Time is significant here. *Twelve* is a number representing a new administration. *Twelve* is the number representing the apostolic gift. The next generation or administration lay dormant, whereas the old administration was pressing through.

When Jesus is ready to move into the new, we who are being taught by Him have the opportunity to respond. The woman with the issue of blood, representing the last season, had to press past her gender issue; she was a woman. She had to press past the law that said that anyone with an issue of blood had to be barred from the public. Then there is always the crowd that one must press through. However, if we press and touch in our desperation, we begin our next new season of life. She was desperate! The Lord acknowledged her and delivered her from her past season and its conflicting religious structure.

Jairus's daughter represented the next administration. He said, "She is not dead, but sleeping" (Luke 8:52). He then commanded her to rise! This was after removing the wailers from the room. The grief of one season must end in order for you to awaken to the next season. The next administration awakened.

The following are eight *new issues* to look for in your life as you move from one season to the next. The following should be reviewed on a quarterly basis by each of us so we stay focused in reaching our destiny:

1. *A new identity.* May His fullness flow through your personality. May your soul be restored. May all fear and manipulation that has crowded your identity and confined you to your past be removed. Your new, transformed personality will have the ability to overcome the mountains in the past season that stopped your progress. (See Isaiah 41; Zechariah 4.)

2. *New garments of favor.* Garments, favor, and identity all go together. When we overcome the circumstances that come into the path of our lives, we develop a testimony. With our testimony comes favor. Favor is much like grace but is

usually linked with our obedience. Favor opens doors. May you overcome, radiate with favor, and have entry way into new opportunities.

3. *New relationships.* When the Lord is doing a new thing in us, we must evaluate all of our relationships. He has new, fresh, divine connections to bring into our paths. He supernaturally aligns us with others who will cause us to come into a greater level of success. He positions people on our path that propel us down our path. One of our most difficult changes in life to make is to let go of certain relationships that will hinder our future. However, when these soul ties are cut, we advance.

4. *New acts.* In the early church, the power of God was displayed through the anointing in Paul's handkerchief and Peter's shadow. Many demonstrations and acts of power through the apostles are recorded. Through history, every time God is ready to do something new, new acts begin that demonstrate His power today. We must expect to see the Lord divinely intervene in our lives with signs, wonders, and miracles in each new season we enter.

5. *New weapons for the war ahead.* With each season we enter we must reevaluate our armor. There are diverse gifts and many operations of those gifts. Our shield of faith must be repaired and shined to remove any wounding from the past season. Our belt of truth must be tightened as we move against new enemies in this age. We must be a people who, like David, choose not to use the proven armor of the last season but to develop our own, which will efficiently overtake the giants in our path.

6. *New sounds.* May you hear the sound of victory and shout this sound from the rooftops. Every new season and every movement is preceded by a new song. We sing before we

develop our theology. New songs break old cycles. Sound creates movement. The trumpet is sounding a new sound. Listen carefully. May you receive everything you need to defeat your enemies

7. *A new anointing.* The anointing breaks the yoke. The anointing makes us grow so that every confining weight falls from us. The anointing, the *mashach*, makes us so greasy that the enemy cannot grasp and hold us from entering into the best that God has for us. May you receive a new anointing! (See Psalm 92.)

8. *A new level of authority.* May you receive the ability to stand in dominion in the sphere of authority that you have been granted by the Lord. May you war and remove every stronghold in that sphere. May you bring every thought captive to the obedience of Christ so you advance and harvest the field He has given you. May your authority be demonstrated by an exercise of power over your enemies that would hinder your progress. (See 2 Corinthians 10.)

THE ANOINTING WILL BREAK OPEN YOUR FUTURE

To stand and withstand we must be anointed. Isaiah 10:27 proclaims that the anointing breaks the yoke. The Hebrew word *mashach* refers to one who is anointed with oil, symbolizing the reception of the Holy Spirit, enabling Him to do an assigned task. Kings (1 Sam. 24:6), high priests, and some prophets (1 Kings 19:16) were anointed. In the case of Cyrus, he was anointed with God's Spirit and commissioned an *anointed deliverer* of Israel (Isa. 45:1). The patriarchs were called "anointed ones."

We need to *receive a new anointing*. This anointing will give you victory over old cycles that are working death in you and will help you overcome the fear of death. You are anointed to have victory over

Anointing will give you victory over old cycles that are working death in you and will help you overcome the fear of death.

demonic forces that would try to stop you from embracing the best the Lord has for you in the future.

May you be anointed for increase and harvest so you begin to fill His storehouse. May you have an Issachar anointing to interpret the times so you know what decisions to make. To *mashach* means "to smear with oil or paint." The hand of the Lord will paint you with His anointing. The enemies of the Lord know you have been set apart.

The following list gives several other uses of the term *anoint* that will broaden your understanding for receiving a new anointing:

1. The anointing represents physical refreshment after washing. In Ruth chapter 3, Ruth made her shift. Naomi told her to take off her widow's garment, wash, and anoint herself. Ruth then went to the threshing floor and found her redeemer. You have toiled too long. I decree that all weariness breaks from you. May His redemptive plan and key connections come clear in your life.

2. *Chrio*, or anoint, is used metaphorically in connection with "the oil of gladness," similar to "a lotion for a sick horse." May the anointing restore your joy. May you be delivered from any form of weakness that could hinder you.

3. The anointing is used to cause eyes that have lost vision to be open again. The church in Laodicea had its eyes anointed with eye salve. May your vision be renewed. May all dead works from the past year be broken. May you receive revelation of new methods that will make you more productive and effective. May a new passion be rekindled.

4. "To rub on" is used for the blind man whose eyes Christ "anointed." May you be healed from any loss of vision or past failures and anointed for your future.

5. *Murizo* is used for "anointing" the body for burial in Mark 14:8. May you receive an anointing, allow the natural death of certain issues that the Lord would like to fall into the ground, and then spring forth in new ways.

6. *Chrisma* means "an anointing from the Holy One" and indicates that this anointing renders them holy, separating them to God. May the Holy Spirit be very efficient in enabling you to possess knowledge of the truth. May this truth unlock the doors that have remained shut to you. May you be separated and favored above the world around you.

7. The anointing means to "grow fat." May every yoke binding you break from around you, and may you go free like a calf let out of a stall.[1]

THE OIL OF ANOINTING

In Monte Judah's article on "The Oil of Anointing," he shares the following:

The olive tree and its fruit are an incredible part of God's creation. The olive tree can withstand incredible damage and still remain alive. In fact, an olive tree can be completely cut off at the base of the ground and still spring up with new branches. The key to the life of the olive tree is its durable root system. Olive trees are indeterminate plants, lasting as long as they continue to receive nourishment. "Sun, stone, drought, silence, and solitude: these are the five ingredients that, according to Italian folk traditions, create the ideal habitat for the olive tree." This is what it takes for us to become who God created us to be.

The olive tree and its fruit is one of the most powerful symbols referred to in the Bible. The tree itself seems to stand as a symbol of the children of Israel themselves. An olive tree can be cut off at the ground and yet survive because of the root. That comparison is readily made of Israel and the root is likened to God's promises. In fact, the national crest of modern Israel is based on the prophecy of Zechariah with his vision of the two olive trees.... The one application of the olive tree and oil that stands out most in all the Bible's applications...is the manifestation of the Messiah. The Hebrew word *Meshiach* is the basis of the title for the Messiah. It literally means "The Anointed One."[2]

Then a shoot will spring from the stem of Jesse, and a branch from his roots will bear fruit. The Spirit of the LORD will rest on Him, the spirit of wisdom and understanding, the spirit of counsel and strength, the spirit of knowledge and the fear of the LORD. And He will delight in the fear of the LORD, and He will not judge by what His eyes see, nor make a decision by what His ears hear; but with righteousness He will judge the poor, and decide with fairness for the afflicted of the earth; and He will strike the earth with the rod of His mouth, and with the breath of His lips He will slay the wicked. Also righteousness will be the belt about His loins, and faithfulness the belt about His waist. And the leopard will lie down with the young goat, and the calf and the young lion and the fatling together; and a little boy will lead them. Also the cow and the bear will graze, their young will lie down together, and the lion will eat straw like the ox. The nursing child will play by the hole of the cobra, and the weaned child will put his hand on the viper's den. They will not hurt or destroy in all My holy mountain, for the earth will be full of the knowledge of the LORD as the waters cover the sea. Then in that day the nations will resort to the root of Jesse, who will stand as a signal for the peoples; and His resting place will be glorious.

—ISAIAH 11:1–10, NASU

Judah also shares, "Is it any wonder that the Messiah taught of the final days to the disciples from the Mount of Olives? It is also noteworthy that when the Messiah did the great work of redemption for us that He went across the Kidron to the Mount of Olives to a garden called Gethsemane. There He prayed, waited, and agonized for what was coming. Gethsemane means the 'olive press.' It is where the olives were first pressed that were harvested from the Mount of Olives. It is where the life of Yeshua was first pressed. The oil of anointing and 'Anointed One' converged there."[3]

We must always find God's pattern of order in the midst of our chaos.

First Kings 6:31–33 says, "For the entrance of the inner sanctuary he made doors of olive wood, the lintel and five-sided doorposts. So he made two doors of olive wood, and he carved on them carvings of cherubim, palm trees, and open flowers, and overlaid them with gold; and he spread the gold on the cherubim and on the palm trees. So also he made for the entrance of the nave four-sided doorposts of olive wood" (NASU).

Judah concludes by sharing:

> Olive trees and olive oil is an important commodity in the world. It is also a powerful practical symbol of our faith in God. The oil of olive is used for anointing, the fuel for the Menorah's light, medicine, food, and for soap. The Messiah is the Anointed One, the light in our darkness, the healing for our lives, the eternal nourishment for our souls, and the soap that cleans us up. To this day the ancient wisdom and understanding of the olive is still with us. Very little has been changed in the word picture from then. Of all the proverbs I have ever heard about olives and olive oil, this is my favorite. When a man has fellowship with another, they sit at a table and break bread together. This is called table fellowship. However, if the fellowship is between the best of friends, they sit at the table, break bread, and eat olives.[4]

A New Order for a Reordered Day

The anointing breaks the yoke and produces new order. We must always find God's pattern of order in the midst of our chaos. My wife, Pam, and

I wrote a whole book about this principle. *One Thing* is a book about remaining simple in a chaotic world, finding your new order, and moving forward into God's best.[5] This principle of God has been revealed from Genesis to Revelation in the Word of God. Because we both had to grasp the principle of restoration in the midst of our chaotic lives, we have learned that every old cycle can be broken and a new order and cycle can begin.

What does *order* mean?

Order means to set a group of objects, persons, or anything else in a straight row. Order occurs when we develop a fixed or definite plan. Order is linked with the law of arrangement and the sequencing of events. Order is a state or condition in which everything is in its right place and functioning properly. Order can also be a command, direction, or instruction. This is a day of commission or forming a request. We are living in an apostolic age in which a new order is forming in the earth. A new government is developing a people commissioned to set order in the world.

We are also living in a time in which the Lord is transforming His people. Order is linked with all the elements that make up our societal structures: architecture, finance, military, science, theology, and politics. There is an order in the government of heaven. There are grades of angels that assist us in doing the Lord's will in the earth. There is a hierarchical structure of demons that resist us. In some forms of religious structures, there is a rank of clergy.

Have you ever been to a Passover *seder* (the ordered arrangement of the meal)? It is also the root of the word *sidur*, the Jewish prayer book that is composed of an ordered arrangement of prayers. The word *seder* is only used one time in the Bible: "The land dark as midnight, (The land) of the shadow of death, without any *order*, and where the light is as midnight" (Job 10:22, ASV, emphasis added).

Seder means order. We must have order in our lives to move from captivity to freedom. We must be ready to move quickly out of bondage. Our movement must gain momentum, and we must keep going until we reach our intended destination.

Another Hebrew word that is used for order is *dor*, or *generation*. A generation is time from one birth to the birth of the next generation. Let me remind you that the Western mind views *time* as linear, as in a timeline, with a beginning and an end. In contrast, the Hebrew mind sees time as a continuous circle. A generation is one circle with each following generation as another circle. These circles connect, or better yet, they overlap the previous circle to produce continuous blessings or cursings in the earth. There is no beginning and no end with the concept of the word *generation*. This circular view of time is perceived as order.

The world also has generations. Genesis 2:4 states, "These are the generations of the heavens and of the earth when they were created" (KJV). The earth has its own generations. Each creation and destruction is one circular generation: the Creation; the fall of man, which was a destruction; Adam and Eve's new life outside of the garden; the flood; and then to Noah and his sons after the flood. Before the flood, the world was full of sin. To bring about order again, the flood came to "weed out" the bad and begin again with a new crop—Noah and his family. Notice the circles of destruction and creation. God is a restorative God who replaces a circle of destruction with a new creative cycle. The end of days will be filled with destruction. The new heavens and new earth will create a new cycle of rule in the earth.

The feminine form of the word *order* is *devorah*, meaning a "bee." A beehive contains a colony of insects that live in a perfectly ordered society. Deborah brought order to a chaotic society that had drifted from the Lord. She also brought order in the midst of war. Her apostolic rule of forty years restored a nation.

Another word that is derived from the concept of order is *midvar*, meaning "wilderness." In the Hebrew mind, the wilderness is a place of order. All organisms of life live in perfect balance and harmony. Our wilderness experiences produce new order in our lives. Think of Jesus's forty-day wilderness experience. He went into the wilderness filled with the Spirit. He resisted every temptation to be known by man. He came out filled with power! The Israelites' forty years of wilderness wanderings reordered a people so that the generation of unbelief was removed.

Do not fear your wilderness; let the Lord reorder your life and remove everything that will hinder your future.

Removing what is unnecessary brings about order to a field so it can be cultivated.

Each of us has a field. When God planted the garden and placed man within the garden, His purpose was for man to cultivate the garden and watch after all activities therein. "And as for all the hills that used to be hoed with a hoe, you will not come there for fear of briers and thorns, but they will become a place where cattle are let loose and where sheep tread" (Isa. 7:25, ESV).

In this passage the "hoed" is the Hebrew *adar*. This is the same word used for Abraham the Hebrew, who crossed over and made covenant with God. As believers, we are grafted into all of Abraham's blessings and receive energy to advance and cross over into the fullness of God's plan in this generation. The concept behind this word is the cultivation of a field and the removal of the weeds so that a crop can grow. Derived from this word is *m'ader*, which indicates "any implement used in hoeing, raking, or digging." Removing what is unnecessary brings order to a field so it can be cultivated. This is an important principle in days ahead for us to harvest the field or sphere of authority that we are each operating in our lives and ministries. We must wait for God's timing to remove the briers, thorns, and tares. There is a perfect time to cultivate our field.

Much warfare is required for breaking old cycles and beginning new. The word *order* is used in the concept of battle. In battle, one must remove fear to be victorious. First Chronicles 12:33 says, "...of Zebulun, such as were able to go out in the host, that could set the battle in array, with all manner of instruments of war, fifty thousand, and that could order (the battle array, and were) not of double heart" (ASV).

In this passage, the phrase "not of double heart" is in the Hebrew *b'lo lev v'lev* and literally translates as "with no heart and heart," but figuratively means "no fear" in the sense that part of their heart was focused on what was at home and the other part of their heart was set on the battle. By removing fear, order is created, and they were able to totally focus with their whole heart on the battle.[6]

TIME AND ORDER

"I have appointed an appointed time!" This would be the best way to describe what the Lord has done at certain moments in our history. There is a "set or space of time" that is appointed and definite! If we are in a season of war and will not submit to the time of war, we will find ourselves confused and lagging behind in the battle.

God appointed evening before morning and determined to release revelation to us that would penetrate the chaos of each day. Each day began at evening with a watch. God wanted us to understand that if we would watch through the night season, He would order our day. Here are the four watches:

- *Evening*—6:00 p.m. to 9:00 p.m. (See Genesis 24:11; Exodus 27:21; Ezra 9:5; Psalm 55:17; Matthew 14:15–23; John 20:19.)

- *Midnight*—9:00 p.m. to 12:00 a.m. (See Exodus 11:4; 12:29; Ruth 3:8; Matthew 25:6; Luke 11:5; Acts 16:25.)

- *Breaking of a day (cock crowing)*—12:00 a.m. to 3:00 a.m. (See Psalm 110; Mark 13:35.)

- *Morning*—3:00 a.m. to 6:00 a.m. (See Exodus 30:7; 34:2; Ruth 3:13–14; Joshua 6:12; 2 Samuel 24:11; Nehemiah 4:21; Mark 1:35, John 21:4.)

There are wonderful happenings that only occur in each watch. Therefore, if the Lord awakens us at 2:00 a.m. to watch with Him for an hour, we should readily respond. That is the time that we will meet God and then He will order our whole day, based upon that one hour of seeking Him. *Reordering Your Day: Understanding and Embracing the Four*

Prayer Watches is a most unusual book that is very helpful for understanding the watches.[7]

In *The Fourth Turning: An American Prophecy* by William Strauss and Neil Howe, they explain that our turnings come in cycles of four.[8] Each cycle spans the length of a long human life that will include a seasonal rhythm of growth, maturation, entropy, and destruction. Each turning has its identifiable mood. Time has always yielded and manifested the same attributes. Each cycle is represented by a circle, symbolizing perfect and unbreakable recurrence. Each circle is divided into phases. Many times we develop rituals to usher in each new circle. There are times of discontinuity and times to restart each creative cycle. Each circle is presumed to repeat itself in the same sequence over a period of similar length. The natural life span is probably the only circle that mankind can neither avoid nor alter. However, we as modern people exercise a freedom to reshape our natural and social environment.[9]

Within all of our life cycles, there are crises. These are decisive or separating moments in time. A crisis can launch you into the next season. If we do not handle our crises properly, they repeat themselves from generation to generation. This is the same principle we find with iniquity. Once an iniquitous pattern is formed, we find it striving to repeat itself so that it holds every generation captive to its twisted thought process. God usually raises up prophets filled with passion to speak into these crises to create a reversal of the destructive workings of our life cycles. Prophets bring God's revelation from heaven into the day in which we live. Any day can be filled with revelation that creates change and causes the earth to reflect the will of heaven. The more we seek God and prophesy, or speak His mind and heart into each day we live, the more we will reflect heaven in the earth realm.

The natural life span is probably the only circle that mankind can neither avoid nor alter.

The Day of the Lord is an interesting phrase that we find in the Word of God. A day can be a twenty-four-hour revolution of time. However, a day can indicate a time period and its reflection of heaven and Earth (Joel 2:2). Biblically, *a day* can mean:

- Day of Atonement (Lev. 23:26–32)

- A time of national cleansing (Rom. 11:25)

- A moment in time when a fountain is opened (Zech. 13:1)

- A moment for a future conversion (Zech. 12:9–14)

- Day of Judgment—a set time of evaluation; the event of the Cross was a day of judgment.

- A day of Christ when we saints receive rewards and blessings (1 Cor. 1:8; 5:5; Phil. 1:6)

- The Day of the Lord, which is the cleansing of heaven and Earth (Rev. 4:1–19:16; Isa. 2:12; 65:16; Rev. 21:1)

- A glorification phase when we experience heaven's glory in Earth's realm.

Let us seek God daily so we can experience the fullness of each day!

THE NARROW PLACE OF TRANSITION

If we are a people of order, we can find our way through every transition. There is an order in crossing over. We have already explained the concept of transition, but now you see that every transition has a timed element and order of progression. Every wilderness you encounter has a forming order that will bring you to a new place. Transitions have very narrow places that make our advancement very difficult. However, unless we make our way through this narrow place, we cannot fulfill our destiny. In our life, we will continue to confront this narrow place over and over until we finally press through into the new.

TRAVAIL IN THE NARROW PLACE

Psalm 127:3 tells us that children are a heritage from the Lord, and the fruit of the womb is a reward. The psalm goes on to say, "Happy is the man who has his quiver full of them; they shall not be ashamed, but shall speak with their enemies in the gate" (v. 5). When it comes to bearing children, it's an interesting fact that there is a desperate, agonizing pain of the soul that comes with barrenness. Equally true, however, is that there is a desperate, travailing pain of the body that comes with giving birth. My wife, Pam, and I understand the agony of barrenness as it was ten years before we were able to have children. There were times of desperation in those years and times we agonized before the Lord. God heard the desperate cries of our hearts for children and brought a miraculous healing to Pam's body that allowed her to conceive. Since that time, she has become familiar with the travailing pain of birth, having given birth to six children. Because what we experience in the natural often mirrors that which we experience in the spiritual, we can see that there are times when agony and travail are appropriate precursors and responses to spiritual birth, just as they are to natural birth. We agonize when something God intends to be has not yet manifested, and we travail as we birth God's new thing into the earth.

When the Lord first spoke this season of travail to me, I was very unclear as to what He was saying. Travail connotes that we are at a narrow transition. This transitional place is a life-and-death intersection. The transitional place is a place of crossing over. I believe we have entered a *season of travail*. *Travail* means that we are in a "distressed" moment. Apostle Barbara Yoder, a dear friend and wonderful leader, sent me this definition of travail: "Travail is a specific type of prayer that both births (Isa. 66:7–9) as well as wars (Isa. 42:12–14). When a person enters a time, period, or season of travail (birthing and/or warring), they will experience it as a heaviness, weight, burden, deep penetrating concern, or unease over a situation or condition that cannot be shaken. Sometimes travail extends to weeks or months, particularly when God burdens a person over a nation."

Travail is defined as birthing; delivering; or being disgusted, faint, grieved, weary, distressed, or troubled. The old Latin word referred to an instrument of torture composed of three stakes to which a person was tied. To *travail* is to be troubled; sorrowful; or in agony, intense pain, or distress. In other words, it is not a comfortable experience. Oftentimes a person will initially interpret *travail* emotionally and become introspective, suspecting something is wrong with himself or herself. However it is not an emotion; it is the burden of the Lord, the voice of the Lord coming to a person as a burden to draw that person into partnering with Him to birth and/or to war.[10]

> *As a person begins to pray, the Holy Spirit takes over and begins to travail within and through that person with groanings that cannot be expressed in English words.*

The only way travail will be released is through prayer. The person will feel weighted down by a situation until it is released through sustained prayer. It is during travail that people often experience a *Romans 8:22–26 time.* The Holy Spirit within a person knows how to pray under this type of burden. As the person begins to pray, the Holy Spirit takes over and begins to travail within and through that person with groanings that cannot be expressed in English words. Isaiah 42:13 says that God Himself "shall go forth like a mighty man; He shall cry out, yes, shout aloud; He shall prevail against His enemies." Verse 14 continues, "I have held My peace a long time, I have been still and restrained Myself. Now I will cry like a woman in labor [travail]."

WHAT SHOULD WE DO NOW?

Here are some keys that will help you to be victorious in this season:

1. *Set aside a time of sanctification. Sanctification* means to "set yourself apart so you are ready to move forward

in God's purpose." Sanctification is a time of removal of impurities. Pray and fast for three days. Ask God for *favor.*

2. *Select seven days for a Jericho confrontation.* The Israelites had to circle for seven days without talking. Let the Lord develop a new sound of victory over the blockade that has seemed invincible in your life.

3. *Be like Mordecai and listen at your gates!* The gates of your life are the most trafficked and influenced places.

4. *Pray for divine recovery.* Make a list of the losses that have affected you most. Decree a new multiplication factor of increase.

5. *Overcome distress and anxiety.* Define what is creating anxiety in you. Praise to prevent anxiety every time you have an anxious thought.

6. *Receive an anointing!* Pray Psalm 92, and anoint yourself. The anointing breaks the yoke.

7. *Be like Hannah!* Do not let those who mock you keep you from pressing through into a new dimension. Travail past your reproach.

HANNAH'S AGONY: AGONIZING PRODUCES CHANGE

One of the most poignant biblical accounts of agonizing before God is the story of Hannah. As the story opens, we see that Israel was in its lowest moral condition as a nation. The priesthood had fallen into total disarray. However, individuals kept coming to Shiloh to offer sacrifices and worship to the Lord. As required by the Law, Elkanah took his entire family to Shiloh to offer sacrifices. Hannah, one of Elkanah's two wives, was barren and unfulfilled. She was a desperate woman because she knew that the destiny of her creation had not been fulfilled. This lack of fulfillment had led her into grief and affliction of spirit, which the Bible calls "bitterness of soul" (1 Samuel 1:10). In verses 11–18 we see how Hannah agonized before the Lord to give her a child. Her agonizing gives us a great pattern to follow:

1. Pray and cry out to the Lord.

2. Weep in anguish (Hannah agonized).

3. Lift your affliction to the Lord.

4. Cry out: "Remember why I was created!"

5. Plead, "Fulfill my request, and You can have my firstfruit offering."

6. Go to the highest-level authority figure in your life who can pray for you. (Hannah told the priest her problem and expressed her emotion.)

7. Ask for favor to come upon you.

8. Press through and then arise in victory.

9. Birth the new thing in your life (and, perhaps, your nation).

10. Watch your travail produce a manifestation.

Through her prayer of agony to the Lord, Hannah conceived and gave birth to Samuel. She then fulfilled her vow to the Lord by giving this child to the priest. This act changed the course of Israel. Samuel began to prophesy, and the nation began to shift, although not everything went well. As the story progresses, we see that Israel was defeated in war and, as a result, lost the ark of the covenant, which represented God's presence among them. This defeat, however, set the nation of Israel on course to restore the presence of God in the land, which David did when he returned the ark to its resting place in Jerusalem many years later.

Travailing Produces Birth

Be in pain, and labor to bring forth,
O daughter of Zion,
Like a woman in birth pangs.
For now you shall go forth from the city,
You shall dwell in the field,
And to Babylon you shall go.
There you shall be delivered;
There the Lord will redeem you
From the hand of your enemies.

—Micah 4:10

Travail is defined as a painfully difficult or burdensome work, particularly the anguish or suffering associated with the labor of childbirth. You may be wondering what that has to do with prayer. If we stop to consider the story of Hannah, we realize that when she approached the Lord, she was in anguish over her circumstances. Her plea to God came from the very depths of her being. Her agony before the Lord did not come purely from the emotion of an unmet need or desire in her life. It rose up out of her spirit because, as we mentioned before, the destiny for which she had been created had gone unfulfilled. (At that time, she did not know in the natural that she had been chosen to give birth to Samuel, a great prophet and judge of Israel.) Somewhere in her spirit, she knew that she could not settle for barrenness. She knew that was not God's portion for her in life.

Before Hannah gave physical birth to Samuel, she travailed for and birthed something spiritually that overcame the curse of barrenness, not only in her own body, but ultimately for the nation of Israel through Samuel. When we travail in prayer, what we are doing is allowing the Holy Spirit to birth something through us. In the nineteenth century, when Charles Finney was pondering travailing prayer, he wrote, "Why does God require such prayer—such strong desires, such agonizing supplications? These strong desires mirror the strength of God's feelings. They are God's real feeling for unrepentant sinners. How strong God's desire must be for His Spirit to produce in Christians such travail—God has chosen the word to describe it—it is travail, torment of the soul."[11]

In her book *Possessing the Gates of the Enemy*, Cindy Jacobs says:

> There are times when we are called by God to pray strong prayers and help to birth the will of God into an area. Usually there is a sense of wonder after the prayer, and a sense that God has done something through it. Here are four points to help you recognize the work of the Holy Spirit:
>
> 1. Travail is given by God and is not something we can make happen. Travail is often a deep groaning inside, which may be audible or which cannot be uttered, as described in Romans 8:26.
>
> 2. Travail sometimes comes as a result of praying in an area that others have prayed about before you. God then chooses you to be one of the last prayers before the matter is accomplished. You are the one who gives birth to the answer.
>
> 3. Those with the gift of intercession will often pray more travailing prayers than those without the gift.
>
> 4. The travail may be short or extended. Some prayers will be accomplished quickly and some will be like labor pangs at different times until the birth of the answer comes.[12]

HOW DOES TRAVAILING PRAYER WORK?

There is a tremendous power in travailing prayer because, as Cindy noted, it births the will of God into the earth. This type of prayer always outwits the devil because he is so strongly opposed by the new thing God is producing as a result of travail. We therefore need to have an understanding of what God wants to birth through us. We, like Hannah, need to be in tune with what God is ready to bring forth in that given hour. That can only be done through intimacy with God and through a willingness to allow Him to use us in travail.

Many times we have much that God has put in our spirits, but we don't have the strength to bring it to birth. Isaiah 60:1 says: "Arise, shine; for your light has come! And the glory of the LORD is risen upon you." In the Amplified Version it says to "ARISE [from the depression and prostration in which circumstances have kept you—rise to new life]!" This is the time to call upon the Lord to begin to break those things that have held down your spirit, for this is the time for the Spirit of God to begin to arise within us. The word *arise* means "to stand firm, to come from a lying-down position to a stand." When we begin to arise and allow God's glory to arise through us, we will take our stand against the powers and principalities that have resisted us. As we allow the Spirit of the Lord to arise within us, we will find that He gives us the expectation of new life and the strength to bring that life to birth.

Travailing prayer always outwits the devil because he is so strongly opposed by the new thing God is producing as a result of travail.

Once this process begins and we identify what burden God wants us to pray over, we begin to agonize and feel the urgency of seeing the burden birthed. The burden becomes our own *baby*, as God's heart for seeing that thing brought forth begins to press down on our spirits. With it comes an oppression, but it's not the oppression of the devil. If your assignment, for instance, is a travail to break an oppression over certain people on God's heart, you can actually begin to feel the oppression they are under. That is the time to travail until the oppression breaks—until, as in natural childbirth, the heavenly opening is large enough so that God's will can come forth on the earth

Linda Heidler, who understands and leads many intercessors through their travail, says, "One of the most interesting passages about wailing is Jeremiah 9:17–18, which says to call for the 'skillful wailing women.' There are three words used for these women. One, *qun*, indicates the sound that they make in their wailing. The second word, *chakam*, is from the root word for wisdom or skill in living. The third word, *nehiy*, means lamentation. Jeremiah 9 describes a time of great national distress.

These women were called to help the nation weep. These women were skilled in releasing the sound that would cause the nation to weep—to grieve over its condition, repent before God, and willingly yield to Him again."[13] We must not fear travail. Men, do not think that travail is only a woman's experience!

SOME CAUTIONS

Because travailing is such an intense and often misunderstood form of prayer, there are some cautions for us be aware of:

1. *Timing.* We cannot enter into travailing prayer on our own any more than a woman can enter into labor before her time. It is something the Holy Spirit chooses to do in His time and through whichever ones of us He chooses, as long as we are open to allowing Him to work travail through us. If we try to bring something to birth before its season, like a baby born prematurely, it is much more susceptible to destruction and death than that which is born in the right season.

2. *Becoming overwhelmed.* Cindy Jacobs gives a good word on this caution: "Many times, travail can be so strong that it seems to overwhelm the intercessor. Those around need to intercede for the one in travail if this happens in a group situation. We need to help bear the burden in prayer.... We also need to bind the enemy from entering into the travail. One word of caution: the Holy Spirit will rule over our emotions in a time of travail. We must be sure that we don't let our emotions run wild. Intercessors need to walk in the fruit of self-control."[14]

3. *Bearing a false burden.* If someone enters travail but does not have God's burden, they will travail with the wind. Isaiah 26:18 says, "We have been with child, we have been in pain; we have, as it were, brought forth wind; we have

not accomplished any deliverance in the earth, nor have the inhabitants of the world fallen." Many well-meaning Christians travail with the wind because they do not understand God's heart in a matter and move forward in presumption. They either do not know or have not taken the time with God to identify with what He is doing. Instead, they go straight into intercession and get lost in it somewhere.

4. *Not completing the assignment.* "This day is a day of trouble, and rebuke, and blasphemy; for the children have come to birth, but there is no strength to bring them forth" (2 Kings 19:3). There are instances in which the timing is right and the burden is right but we have no strength to bring forth the new birth. We must not grow weary in spirit, but allow God to bring forth the strength we need to complete our travail.

MOVING INTO THE JUBILEE SEASON

A woman, when she is in labor, has sorrow because her hour has come; but as soon as she has given birth to the child, she no longer remembers the anguish, for joy that a human being has been born into the world. Therefore you now have sorrow; but I will see you again and your heart will rejoice, and your joy no one will take from you.

—JOHN 16:21–22

We have not been designed to stay in the place of travail either physically or spiritually. We have been designed to bring forth new birth and then move into the new season of life that birth brings to us. After travail comes release. God has a jubilee season over every issue. For instance, if the issue you have been in travail for deals with financial supply, when release comes, God will give you or whomever you have been travailing for incredible strategies over how to break debt structures to see increase and supply begin to flow. That usually includes two arenas. First, there is a physical, financial arena. God will give strategic insight over how to be released from debt and increased for future advancement. Second, there is a relationship arena. If you or the one you have been travailing for have relationships that are broken, that is also a type of debt. God can begin to find supernatural ways to heal those relationships and cause them to flourish.

During a year of jubilee, there is a suspension of labor. The difficult things that you have been travailing for in the past—those things that have been so hard and unyielding, and yet in which you have faithfully pressed through—suddenly come forth and you are released from your hard labor. It is then that you enter into a joy and a faith that you didn't have, and many things start falling into place as a new order begins to come. As we agonize, travail, and labor for those things that God has laid on our hearts, remember there is a time when the birth comes and we are able to enter into our season of jubilee.[15]

God will give strategic insight over how to be released from debt and increased for future advancement.

WE WILL NARROWLY ADVANCE

There are times in our lives when we must advance and move forward. As we have already seen, the Israelites had to move into a new land. For us, this advance could be in a new land or a new job or, in actuality, anyplace that is unfamiliar or new in our lives. At every new level there is a new devil, or two, or seven! Therefore, we must find our footing on how to advance.

Joshua had been mentored for forty years by Moses. However, Moses had never been in the land that Joshua now found himself facing. Moses had heard of the giants in this land but never had seen them. Now Joshua was facing them. The first issue was to ready a people to meet the challenges ahead. There are many examples of how to move through a narrow place, but we must remember to move slowly in new places so we find our footing. God had said through Moses that they would take the land little by little (Deut. 7:22).

Here is how God led them. They came to Gilgal, and the Lord told them to stop and become vulnerable before Him (Josh. 5). In the land of the enemy they were to become so vulnerable before the Lord that they could only trust Him and not their flesh. *Gilgal* means to "roll away." To move forward, they had to stop for a time of circumcision—a cutting away of the reproach of the past! This is always necessary if we are to advance into our future. The *reasons* for our wilderness, not the *lessons* of the wilderness, must be cut away. If not, we will never make it through our narrow place. Here are some other examples and actions necessary for advancing through a narrow place:

- Fast—seek God for help on the road ahead (Ezek. 8).

- Embrace a day of conception, birthing, and jubilation (1 Sam. 1–2).

- Legislate the heavenlies (1 Kings 18).

- Do not miss your day of desperation (Matt. 9).

- Press out everything that could keep you from completing your mission (Luke 9:51; Luke 22:39; John 18).

- Be confident that there is a day of overcoming (Rev. 12).

To assist you in making transitions, here is a prayer focus that could change your life. The discipline of being focused in prayer is like placing a magnifying glass over dried leaves and allowing the sun's beams to align so that eventually a fire begins. The same thing happens when we focus our prayers. Eventually, we burn away the dross that is preventing us from moving forward into the next place. We are retimed by God and advance!

PRAYER FOCUS: TEN DAYS TO MOVE FROM TRAVAIL TO OVERCOMING

Day 1

Read Genesis 31–35. Jacob moved from being a "supplanter" to a "contender with God." Ask the Lord to reveal the areas where He wants you to contend and birth in a new way.

Day 2

Sanctify yourself. Cross over into the *new*. Allow the Lord to bring you to a *new vulnerable place*! Read Joshua 3–5.

Day 3

Go up against your "Jericho" by the Spirit. Read Joshua 6. Memorize Isaiah 30:15.

Day 4

Study the story of Hannah. Embrace a day of conception, birthing, and jubilation! Read 1 Samuel 1–3.

Day 5

Fast and seek God for help on your road ahead! There comes a time for the Lord to cause you to wait. Read Ezra 8, especially verse 21. Do not go any further without a reevaluation of your path.

Day 6

Ask the Lord to teach you to *legislate the heavenlies!* Read 1 Kings 17–18. (Also, look at the first ten verses of 1 Kings 19, and do not let the enemy push you out of your abiding place.)

Day 7

Receive new *favor*! Read Isaiah 60–61. Read Luke 1. Sing or listen to a new song! Exalt the Lord!

Day 8

Embrace a day of desperation! Be like the woman who pressed through. Read Matthew 9 and Romans 8.

Day 9

The most incredible example of travail is Jesus in the Garden of Gethsemane, "the Oil Press." Press out everything that could keep you from completing your mission! Read Luke 9:51, John 18, and Luke 22:39.

Day 10

Plead the blood of Jesus over what you are bringing forth new in your life. Embrace a *day of overcoming*! Declare that your enemy is overcome. Read Revelation 12.

CHAPTER 8

MAKING IT THROUGH
NARROW TRANSITIONS

HAVE YOU EVER GOTTEN TO A PLACE AND TIME IN YOUR LIFE where you did not know how to move forward? I am not talking about being on a dead-end street but more of taking one of the two paths that diverged in the woods (as the poem by Robert Frost goes) and then not knowing how to advance on your path when it gets dark.

Here is another situation: You get to a place in your life where you know you need change, but you are not certain what course in life to take, so you secure the change. You might not feel very good about where you are, but you are not sure of where you are going, so passivity and fear compete to hold you in a stagnant place.

Then there are the times when so many circumstances overwhelm you that you know you can't remain in the crisis mode of life any longer and are willing to make a move—any move—even if it's a wrong move. You are so confused that you are willing to try anything. These are all normal feelings and impulses when we are in transition. In days ahead, we will go through many transitions, but we must learn to keep going, enter and get established in the new, and keep going. We must understand our times and seasons and know what to do in order to advance with a spirit of excellence and an attitude of triumph.

Sandie Freed, a good friend and a great author, writes the following in "Times of Transition—Breakthroughs in New Ways":

> The Church is in a season of "transition." In the Webster's dictionary, *transition* is defined as "moving from one place to another or moving from one position to another." Also, transition is defined as moving

from one *concept* to another. Transition involves moving from one revelation to another level of revelation. A concept is an idea, principle, or a thinking process. Spiritually, when we move from one "concept" to another, it is actually moving from "one revelation to a new revelation!" This implies that during any season of great transition, we are moving forward with new truth, understanding, and wisdom. The main purpose of transition and the receiving of the new revelation is to *embrace* the disclosure of the mystery that was once hidden but is now revealed to us! We must not treat the new revelation frivolously; it must be considered a "holy thing" to us. When we are keeping a new revelation "holy," it means that we protect it, guard it, and separate it unto the Lord. We cannot allow the new revelation to be defiled by the old, (old lifestyles, old belief systems, mind-sets, etc.) therefore, we must consider it holy.[1]

We get so familiar with sound that when God brings down a new sound to create a new style in us, we often prefer the old and resist embracing the new.

When I think of transition, I think of a changing stage in a play. That is the way our life is actually evolving. We are moving from one act to another to another, until the final curtain drops on a season of our life. Another way to think of transition is to remember taking a course in school and think of the course curriculum. We are moving from one subject to another until we finally finish a season and graduate with a certificate of completion. We do not know it all and must be willing to learn. Get ready for your next course!

Transition also means change in movement or development. It means that there is an evolution from one form or stage or style to another. Your body moves with and responds to sound. Remember the Book of Joel? When God was ready to reverse the four stages of destruction, He said, "Blow the trumpet in Zion!" We get so familiar with sound that when God brings down a new sound to create a new style in us, we often prefer the old and resist embracing the new; we convince ourselves that we don't want our body to move in a new way to a new sound. Then we will miss the revelation that God has brought down with the sound.

A Transition Produces a Quantum of Energy

I have really enjoyed reading the book *Vertical Leap* by Al Hollingsworth.[2] Al uses the premise of Proverbs 23:7: "For as he thinketh in his heart, so is he" (KJV). Hollingsworth writes: "When you feel inferior on the inside, you lose power on the outside. We want to push the inside out. That is *Vertical Leap*. Jesus did not wait for conditions on the outside to affect Him on the inside. He already had an agenda on the inside. Logic rebels against faith. Jesus healed the sick and raised the dead. That is not logical."[3]

In every transition you must rely upon the strength within you to get to the other side of where you are going. We transition to produce miracles. At every key transition or crossing-over place of my life, there are four things I do:

1. Praise.

Praise the LORD!

Sing to the LORD a new song,
And His praise in the assembly of saints.

Let Israel rejoice in their Maker;
Let the children of Zion be joyful in their King.
Let them praise His name with the dance;
Let them sing praises to Him with the timbrel and harp.
For the LORD takes pleasure in His people;
He will beautify the humble with salvation.

Let the saints be joyful in glory;
Let them sing aloud on their beds.
Let the high praises of God be in their mouth,

And a two-edged sword in their hand,
To execute vengeance on the nations,
And punishments on the peoples;
To bind their kings with chains,
And their nobles with fetters of iron;
To execute on them the written judgment—
This honor have all His saints.

Praise the LORD!

—PSALM 149

So many times we forget to praise the One who loves us, who is watching after us and longing for us to experience His best. When we praise, He inhabits! His Spirit comes and seats Himself on the throne of our hearts and begins to work His way in us until it is seen around us. This incredible weapon of praise gives us great authority as we face uncertain times and a future in which God is expecting us to end better than we began.

2. Read the Word.

Hebrews 4:12 says, "For the word of God is living and powerful, and sharper than any two-edged sword, piercing even to the division of soul and spirit, and of joints and marrow, and is a discerner of the thoughts and intents of the heart." Ask the Lord to illuminate His Word to energize you, give you direction, cut away the old, and unlock the best that is for you in days ahead. I not only read the Word, but I also meditate on the Word. The Word working in our lives will change our minds.

3. Embrace God's identity for me in the future.

I try to let go of old expectations, relationships, and revelation that are not pertinent to my future. Great prophetic acts in the past will not open up the heavens now. We must hear and act today. Isaiah 41:15–20 is another wonderful passage of Scripture, especially verse 15: "You will be a new threshing instrument with many sharp teeth. You will tear your enemies apart, making chaff of mountains" (NLT). You have a changing identity. Remember that all the failures of your past can change with one act of faith today. Embrace your identity for the future so you can thresh or overcome all the obstacles that defeated you or blocked your way in the past. Do not forget that the Lord Jesus Christ is a sword (Isa. 49:2; Rev. 1:16). May you come into a new, intimate place with Him and overcome and press through into a new identity.

4. Give.

When I do not know what to do in any situation, I ask the Lord one question: "What would You have me give?" This was Father's pattern of victory and defeat of His enemy. This was how Father redeemed you, me, and all of mankind—He gave His Son! Giving unlocks our love, causes our faith to work, and produces a weapon that startles the enemy. When I hear Him tell me what to give, everything else I am seeking to hear from Him falls into place.

> *All the failures of your past can change with one act of faith today.*

In *Vertical Leap* Hollingsworth goes on to say, "Time is a measurement of one's conscious awareness. In one's consciousness, time is observed as a measuring tool. A dead man is not conscious of time. In order for objects to be differentiated, there must be space that separates them. The space between objects is the distance from one object to another. This distance of space can be measured by time. Space exists with conscious time measurement. Within space exists all the things we perceive with our senses. So within our consciousness exists time, space, and things. Since the kingdom of God is within us, we do not need to chase and desire the things on the outside of us, but we must return to that which is within us and 'seek the kingdom of God, and His righteousness, and all things will be added unto us' (Matt. 6:33)."[4]

From this invisible kingdom that defies space and time, we can grasp the best that God has for us and make it through every transition into our future.

TRANSITIONAL SNARES

We are all in different places. Some are dying, some are confused, and some are at a new beginning. That is why we need each other. If you are dying or dying to something, you need comfort. If you are confused or in the process of changing from one thought pattern to another, you need to have strategy and wisdom. If you are beginning, say, "God, help me; I'm starting over again!"

The mind is enmity with God. I will write much about this in the next book in this series. The way our mind perceives something can control our emotions and block our spirit man so we have no strength to make our way through transition. When revelation comes into our lives, our categorized information and actions from the past season resist the change and challenge the new. Transition is a passage! Therefore, we must get rid of some old information to receive the new that has been revealed. Transitions have narrow places. We must take off or remove what we have been carrying in the past season to get through into the next season.

There are things on your path that are designed to stop you from moving forward. There are many snares listed in the Bible. Three-fourths of the people in the Bible who became ensnared made the faith chapter, so don't think that just because you were ensnared you won't make it! Here are some transitional snares to watch for in your time of change.

Sarah

Sarah got tired of waiting to have a baby. She got tired of waiting to conceive. She heard the promise of the Lord and decided to orchestrate that promise through the arm of the flesh by giving her servant Hagar to Abraham so they could bring forth the promise. Hagar got pregnant. When the baby was born, Sarah realized what she had done. Once her act manifested about a year later (your acts do not always manifest immediately), her mistake was evident to her. Did this mean she could not regroup? Absolutely not! If you have fallen into the snare of not waiting, ask God to deliver you. Sarah, the first woman we find in the faith chapter, regrouped, grew "hot" at an old age, and conceived. The snare of not waiting is not irrevocable but does have consequences. Sarah's snare still has consequences today. Psalm 27:14 says: "Wait on the Lord; be of good courage, and He shall strengthen your heart; wait, I say, on the Lord!"

Lot's wife

Her snare was that she loved the mess of sin she was living in and refused God when He brought a way of escape! When God sent angels to get Lot, their two daughters, and her out of that sin, she did not heed the angels' warning and looked back. If you do not let go of what God says to let go of, you will look back, and your desires will be for your past rather than for your future. Lot's wife turned to salt. Salt was a symbol of covenant. Her hardness was an example of not trusting and walking in covenant.

Israel in the wilderness

We are a dangerous people who have great influence. Our opinions matter to each other. Murmuring and complaining is contagious. If you murmur and complain, God will have to do something. This is one way to get God's attention. If you murmur and complain, He will come down, but He won't do the same thing as when you are trying to touch His heart and bring in His presence. Murmuring and complaining is like a rotten apple in a barrel. Remember, the Hebrew people came out of Egypt supernaturally. They traveled three days into the wilderness and started murmuring and complaining. That is like us. We get out on Friday, do OK over the weekend, and then start up again on Monday. This Egyptian mindset must shift if we are to advance into all that God has promised. The Lord came down and said, "I am the Lord who heals you" (Exod. 15:26).

If you do not let go of what God says to let go of, you will look back, and your desires will be for your past rather than for your future.

Murmuring and complaining brought the character of Jehovah *Rophe* from heaven into their atmosphere. We must be healed of murmuring and complaining. Forty years later, only a few of them made it into the original promise. They had been snared by the words of their mouth.

Moses

When the Israelites needed water, God told Moses to strike the rock with his rod and bring forth water. The next time the people were thirsty and needed water, He told Moses to speak to the rock and bring forth water. Remember Moses's snare. He said that he could not lead the people because he could not talk. At this point, God was telling him to reflect a pattern of heaven and overcome his insecurity. Instead of Aaron talking or Moses using his rod, God wanted him to speak. There comes a time when God says we will either use what we do not want to use, or we will not be able to use it again. Moses allowed the people to provoke him to anger. Moses was denied entrance into the destined Promised Land.

How many of you know that if you throw a fit just because everyone is driving you crazy, God may not overlook your action? When you try to blame it on someone else, He does not listen to you. Remember, insecurity is no more than pride. We think it is so sweet to say, "Oh, I can't do that." God knows what you are capable of doing. If He says to do it, you can do it. You might not do it well the first time, but you can start somewhere. That is called a new beginning. New beginnings are not refined. That is why we usually do not step into them. They are never in order. They are usually a mess, but it is a new beginning. Moses's snare was to defy the pattern of heaven and rely upon what had worked in the past. Always try the new thing the Lord is asking of you.

Gehazi

He did not make his transition well. He was Elisha's servant. His snare was to covet something that he should not have had. His story is linked with Naaman, the military leader of Syria who had leprosy. Naaman had an Israelite slave girl living in his home who gave him some wonderful advice. She told him that if he would go to Israel, the prophet Elisha would heal him. Syria and Israel were enemies. Naaman may not have wanted to go to Israel, but he went anyway. Elisha told him to dunk himself in the Jordan River, not in a Syrian river. Naaman balked at the thought of dunking himself in his enemy's river. Some of us will not make our transitions because we will not do something we do not want to do. Eventually, Naaman did what Elisha said and dunked himself in the river. It was a prophetic act of Syria, the enemy, submitting. When he came up healed, he offered all kinds of riches to Elisha. He refused the riches, knowing there was a snare if he received them. Gehazi, his servant, was not as wise and did not follow the model of his master. Gehazi took what had been refused. God saw that Gehazi usurped the authority to which he should have been loyal; Gehazi's desires overruled his loyalty. (See 2 Kings 5.)

In your transitions, this is a great snare. Be careful that your own desires, which are always linked to greed, do not overrule the authority structure you are in and that you do not wrongly move forward trying to receive something you are not to have. Gehazi not only received the riches, but he also got the disease of Naaman.

Peter

We can all relate to Peter. He was an emotional, quick-response individual. In Matthew 16, he had just connected with the Father and declared the true identity of Jesus. This caused Jesus to respond by prophesying to him that the church would be built on this revelation. He went on to say that we would be given the authority to bind and loose and that the keys to the kingdom would be released to us. Jesus then began to talk about going to Jerusalem, being killed, and rising in three days. Peter rose up with all of the emotion that sounds so spiritual and effectively said, "You can't do that!" (See Matthew 16:21–23.) Jesus rebuked Peter and actually equated him to Satan. Your emotions can keep people from obeying. Satan was occupying Peter's emotions. If we do not keep our emotions submitted to the Holy Spirit, Satan will occupy them. Your emotions and human reasoning can be a snare to your advancement.

Thomas

Thomas was a good man, but he could not believe that the Lord had been resurrected—even though the Lord had prophesied that this would happen. I wonder how many times we disciples, or learners, hear the Word and then lose sight of what has been said. Thomas let his unbelief and doubt manifest. He could not believe! The Lord made him touch the scars that resulted from His crucifixion when He was put to death. The Lord told him that it would have been better to believe without seeing and touching. There is no faith if you have to see it, and without faith it is impossible to please God. During every transition, keep your shield of faith intact and you will please God as you make your journey forward.

There are many others who had to navigate transitional snares. The Bible shows us many individuals who have doubted, denied, gotten confused, made wrong decisions, and yet advanced into the fullness of His purpose. We could remember Mary and Martha. They had a very difficult time with Jesus's timetable when their brother fell ill and died. The Lord said to them, "If you would believe you would see the glory of God" (John 11:40). We could remember Saul who became Paul. The Damascus-road experience changed his direction, and he made his transition from being a persecutor to the lead apostle of his day. There is a way through every transition. Watch for snares, and proceed. We will discuss the battle of the conscious and subconscious mind in the next book, *Redeeming the Time*.

ISSACHAR: THE TRIBE THAT UNDERSTOOD TIME AND KNEW WHAT TO DO

Issachar was the ninth son of Jacob and the fifth son of Leah. This birth order possesses properties found in no other number. The number nine, or *tet* in Hebrew, means to judge, bring to judgment, administer justice, adjudicate, execute judgment, rule, or govern. Actually, this number is linked with the concept of goodness.[5] One aspect of Issachar we find in the New Testament is linked to the fruit of the Spirit and the gifts of the Spirit. There are nine of each. To know what to do in a situation, we must allow the gift of the Holy Spirit to manifest within us. If we do this, we will profit in all things (1 Cor. 12:7).

The number five, or *hei* in Hebrew, connotes strength, protection, deliverance, and exaltation. The best scripture to represent the Hebraic concept linked with the number five is Psalm 118:14: "The LORD is my strength and song, and He has become my salvation." The usual translation is "song," but its second meaning is "praise" or "the object of praise." A third meaning is "choice things," a fourth meaning is "to prune, cut off, or pinch off," and a fifth meaning is "strength, power, or protection." The overall concept of the number five is receiving grace to help.[6]

When the power of grace enters into time, many situations are rearranged. There is not an understanding of the full concept of judgment in the body of Christ. When God is ending one season and beginning another, or taking us through transition, He has to end or bring to death some old situations. This is why the tribe of Issachar could understand time. They knew how certain structures had to end so that the new season that God had would begin.

The tribe of Issachar was positioned strategically with Judah and Zebulun (Num. 2:5; 10:14–15). *Zebulun*, the tenth son of Jacob and the sixth and last of Leah, meant "dwelling, habitation." Zebulun was the tribe of war, ships, and trade. Judah was the fourth son of Jacob and Leah. His name meant "may He [God] be praised." Judah prophetically was always destined to go first as the war tribe that would conquer. You can see now why the famous scripture from 1 Chronicles 12:32, "And of Issachar, men who had understanding of the times to know what Israel ought to do, 200 chiefs; and all their kinsmen were under their command" (AMP), had such significance at the time. The tribes were in a tremendous conflict and transition. The government was changing. They were moving from the government of the house of Saul to the government of the house of

Walk in the ability to discern the Spirit's timings and leadings and the Holy Spirit will faithfully reveal to you the times and seasons.

David. David was of Judah. Issachar could give great insight on how to make this shift. The Issachar tribe had several distinct characteristics in its DNA. These include:

1. Prosperity

> Now Reuben went at the time of wheat harvest and found some mandrakes (love apples) in the field and brought them to his mother Leah. Then Rachel said to Leah, Give me, I pray you, some of your son's mandrakes. But [Leah] answered, Is it not enough that you have taken my husband without your taking away my son's mandrakes also? And Rachel said, Jacob shall sleep with you tonight [in exchange] for your son's mandrakes. And Jacob came out of the field in the evening, and Leah went out to meet him and said, You must sleep with me [tonight], for I have certainly paid your hire with my son's mandrakes. So he slept with her that night.
>
> And God heeded Leah's [prayer], and she conceived and bore Jacob [her] fifth son. Leah said, God has given me my hire, because I have given my maid to my husband; and she called his name Issachar [hired].
>
> —GENESIS 30:14–18, AMP

The people of the tribe of Issachar would become servants to many, work for wages, and live a comfortable life.

2. Intercession

Jacob's prophecy in Genesis 49:14–15 says, "Issachar is a strong-boned donkey crouching down between the sheepfolds. And he saw that rest was good and that the land was pleasant; and he bowed his shoulder to bear [his burdens] and became a servant to tribute [subjected to forced labor]" (AMP). The ability to stand between two burdens or two decisions and choose correctly was a quality of this tribe.

3. Divine alignment

The tribe of Issachar moved at home and abroad in its sphere of authority. Moses, in Deuteronomy 33:18–19, puts the tribes of Issachar and Zebulun together as he prophesies: "About Zebulun he said: 'Rejoice, Zebulun, in your going out, and you, Issachar, in your tents. They will summon peoples to the mountain and there offer sacrifices of righteousness; they will feast on the abundance of the seas, on the treasures hidden in the sand'" (NIV). In other words, Zebulun would trade and Issachar would manage at home what was traded (Isa. 60:5–6, 16; 66:11–12; Deut. 4:13–16).

4. Ability to ascertain seasonal and immediate changes in time

The men of Issachar knew how to ascertain the periods of the sun and moon and could interpret times and seasons. This allowed them to understand the land (Deut. 20:11; 1 Kings 9:21). Most of the fertile Valley of Jezreel, or Esdraelon, fell within Issachar's territory. Its fertile, flat plains were well suited for the raising of cattle.[7]

According to the Targum, this meant that they not only knew how to ascertain the periods of the sun and moon, but also the intercalation of months and the dates of solemn feasts so they could interpret the signs of the times. A company from Issachar came to the celebration of the Passover when it was restored by Hezekiah (2 Chron. 30:18). Issachar has a portion assigned to him in Ezekiel's ideal division of the land (Ezek. 48:25); and he also appears in the list in Revelation 7:7.[8] Issachar was destined to stand and occupy the place that Ahab and Jezebel ruled, Jezreel.

5. Awareness of the anointing

Isaiah 10:27 says, "The yoke will be destroyed because of the anointing oil." An Issachar type of gifting recognizes what is necessary to break people free from their bondage. If we receive this anointing and remember where we are called to stand, we can see the overthrow of every Jezebel structure that has risen against God's kingdom plan in our generation. The danger is that we will lose our sense of timing with our footing or become comfortable in our prosperity and allow Jezebel to take our destined valley.

6. Understanding of war and political change

You find the tribe Issachar moving with Deborah and Barak in battle. In spite of its reputation for seeking comfort, the tribe did fight bravely against Sisera (Judg. 5:15). I would have to say that I have walked and also tried to lead the body in the quest to understand the political changes we are experiencing and how to abound in the midst of political upheaval and war around us.

7. Possession of the power to bless

In the unusual circumstance at Shechem in Joshua 10, Issachar was chosen as one of the tribes that could bless what God was blessing. Those who know how to bless get blessed.

Spiritually, Christians are men "knowing the time, that now it is high time to awake out of sleep; for now our salvation is nearer than when we first believed" (Rom 13:11; cf. Eph. 5:16; 1 Pet. 4:1–4). We should help transfer the kingdom from Satan to its coming rightful Lord (Luke 19:12–27). Jerusalem fell "because you did not know the time of your visitation" (Luke 19:44). They are truly wise who turn many from the power of Satan unto God (Dan. 12:3; Acts 26:18).[9] Because we are grafted into the covenant of Abraham and the fullness of the Jew and Gentile must occur before the Lord returns to the earth to reign, we need to receive this anointing and be like this tribe.

Reviewing the above characteristics of Issachar, we could ascertain that Issachar would have a snare for comfort rather than war. They would also be prone to move in "sun worship" instead of prophecy. However, this tribe had the ability to move in and understand feast times and position themselves at the right place at the right time. God is raising up this tribe again in the earth.

BIBLICAL PATTERNS TO SET YOUR SPIRITUAL CLOCK

In the positioning of the tribes for movement and war around the tabernacle, we find Issachar is on the east with Judah and Zebulun. I am attentive to His presence and Issachar's relation to it. In Tim Hegg's notes on "HaShem—Bringing Us Into His Abode," we find the following:

> In this final *parashah* of *Shemot* (Exodus) we are struck by the repeated refrain "according to all that God had commanded, so they did" (or something similar). No less than 18 times in our text for this Shabbat is it noted that the people and Moses did just as the Lord commanded. Perhaps never before, and never again (until the return of Messiah), will the nation of Israel be whole like it was at this time to operate obediently and advance with power. What is to be derived from this remarkable emphasis? What should we learn from it?
>
> First, the conclusion of *Shemot* is clearly focused to teach us that the primary purpose of the Exodus and of the tabernacle with its services and priesthood was that God should dwell among His people. Here, in our section, we have the crowning event, the descending of the Shekinah, God's dwelling presence, to fill the tabernacle with the glory of God. The glory, which had been displayed upon the mountain in the sight of Moses, Aaron, and the others, would now come to dwell in and over the Tabernacle so that all could see His presence. Now we understand why the oft-repeated phrase of Israel's obedience to God's commandments in constructing the tabernacle is found here: preparing a place for God's presence begins with the obedience of His people.
>
> These expressions would indicate that the people had a genuine desire for companionship with God. The principle of the tithe attaches to the issue of "things," while the appointed times (Sabbath and festivals) attach to the matter of our "time." Would we have been willing to give up our savings account in order to prepare the *Mishkan*, a place for God's *Shekinah*? Would we have conformed our schedules to match God's requirements? It is very interesting that God prescribes exactly when the *Mishkan* was to be erected: "On the day of the first new moon, on the first of the month." God asks us to demonstrate the level of our desire for His presence by submitting to Him the two things we value the most: our material possessions and our time.... God dwells among those who put Him

first—who desire His presence above all else....A fourth element I wish to emphasize as we see the manner in which the people prepared for the *Shekinah* is that they were ready to be led by the *Shekinah*. It is one thing to sacrifice and prepare for the presence of the Lord and another thing to commit oneself to following wherever the presence of God leads.[10]

Telling time is a skill we learn. However, interpreting the times is a gift. God ordained the people to understand how to operate around the feast times if they were to move in sync with Him. I will discuss this at length in *Redeeming the Times*.

In understanding the times, every month is key to understand as we pray and seek God within a given year. Each month of the Hebrew calendar is linked with a tribe. The first month is associated with Judah, who goes first. *Judah* means "praise," and praise should be preeminent in our lives. The first month includes Passover. You say, "Well, I thought the first month began with January." In our Western culture and on the Roman calendar you are correct. However, we must see God's pattern of movement in the earth. Passover is linked with redemption. During the first month, you go into a redemptive season in which God has a plan for you to advance. Redemption means that the Lord has already paid your way out of prison. That is the good news! He went to the cross, shed His blood, and paid your way out of the prison you were in. This allows you to find your way out of anything that is confining you. Whether it is an emotional issue or a physical issue, this month you can say, "My freedom has been paid for."

Confrontation is a key in this first month. Think of how God was using Moses to make a decree and then confront the spiritual forces linked with the ruling idolatry in Egypt. Remember that in every season you must be willing to confront what is blocking your way from moving forward and worshiping the Lord in the way He is calling you to worship Him. You might have to look your enemy in the face and speak a hard word like Moses did to Pharaoh. Moses actually exhibited the love of God to Pharaoh, giving him opportunity after opportunity to change.

The Passover month reminds us that confrontations and decrees will liberate us from bondage and break us into our future.

Another thing you can expect in the first month is a supernatural release of joy. Joy is an expression of emotion and is also linked with a release of our will. There is a supernatural joy you can expect in the first month because the enemy's plan will be overturned. You need to expect any strategy of hell to be overturned. Psalm 8:1–4 says this is a month when the Lord is setting a wedge over us. What a wedge does is open something or hold something back. Think of the people in Egypt. God "wedged open" the Red Sea, then held the army of Egypt back so the Israelites could make it through. Then He overtook Egypt. That is a good picture to remember for the first month, and it helps us tell time and move forward. I will explain much more of this concept in the next book.

Redemption means that the Lord has already paid your way out of prison.

THE IDEA OF REVELATION

Revelation causes obscure things to become clear and brings hidden things to light. Revelation shows signs that will point us into our path of destiny. Revelation is timed from Father and made accessible and available to us by the Son and implemented by the Spirit of God. Without revelation, we go backward, lose our way, and eventually find ourselves on a wrong path. There is a river of revelation available to us. We can boldly enter the throne room of God! God revealed His name to us. We are named after Him (Deut. 28:10). We are different from other groups seeking to know their Creator. We are grafted into the Abrahamic covenant. That covenant was fulfilled when Jesus obeyed the Father and was sacrificed for our sin. We have now been given recorded revelation that is relevant today. Not only can man seek a relationship with God, but also we are the only people in the earth who can seek God and experience the Spirit of God in the earth. We have the Word of God to align our thoughts and desires with a Holy God who created us and will visit with us over our destiny. The Word is not just wisdom—the Word is destiny! God has disclosed His will to some men for all men.

The Word answers the most important question: what does God demand of us? As we seek God on a daily basis, we can answer this question. To most of us, the idea of daily revelation is unacceptable, not because it cannot be proved or explained, but because it is unprecedented. Many times what we hear from the Lord to uncover what has not been disclosed is *new*—not new in the sense of the recorded Word, but new in the thought of God coming into our space today.

We must not reject God's perfect will revealed through revelation. Often those thoughts are so different from the world's way of doing things that the revelation seems contrary and simply does not enter our minds. Our minds can be so conformed to the world that we possess no form or category of understanding for an idea that just came as an impression into our spirit to take hold of.

To most of us, the idea of daily revelation is unacceptable, not because it cannot be proved or explained, but because it is unprecedented.

From early childhood, we are trained to explain rationally all that happens in our little world around us. Happenings are seen as part of the overall laws and physics structure that we live in. Therefore, when the extraordinary happens, we relegate the happening to circumstance or coincidence. However, there are many times when the Spirit of God is intervening in our lives! Angelic operations preempt and stop many detrimental circumstances that could keep us from completing our destiny. We are entering a season when we must be able to perceive the intervention of a God who loves us and wants the best for us. We must also be capable of discerning when evil is in operation against God's best plan. We are made in His image to commune with Him, see what He sees, and experience Him when He is near to us.

We have become so used to living in a natural world that we have taken on a humanistic approach to life. Science must align with the

Word of God as He reveals it to us. The Word of God does not align with scientific thinking that says, "If something unique happens in your space and time, there must be a way it can be re-created and happen again." God is unique, diverse, and creative in His ability to reveal Himself to mankind. All revelation is unique in that it comes at a moment in time in this age—a totally unique event. We do not live in the history of the Word, but yet the Word is revealed to us today so that we might walk in freedom and represent Him in the earth. Creative ability comes to those who can capture the unique thought process of God in a moment's flash. Those are the people in the earth that produce a change in history.

STAND AND WITHSTAND

We must learn to stand and withstand.

> Finally, my brethren, be strong in the Lord and in the power of His might. Put on the whole armor of God, that you may be able to stand against the wiles of the devil. For we do not wrestle against flesh and blood, but against principalities, against powers, against the rulers of the darkness of this age, against spiritual hosts of wickedness in the heavenly places. Therefore take up the whole armor of God, that you may be able to withstand in the evil day, and having done all, to stand. Stand therefore, having girded your waist with truth, having put on the breastplate of righteousness, and having shod your feet with the preparation of the gospel of peace; above all, taking the shield of faith with which you will be able to quench all the fiery darts of the wicked one. And take the helmet of salvation, and the sword of the Spirit, which is the word of God; praying always with all prayer and supplication in the Spirit, being watchful to this end with all perseverance and supplication for all the saints.
>
> —EPHESIANS 6:10–18

James 4:7–8 admonishes us to, "Submit to God. Resist the devil and he will flee from you. Draw near to God and He will draw near to you.

Cleanse your hands, you sinners; and purify your hearts, you double-minded." So, for us to stand, we must submit. The word *submit* means "to stand under." The word *stand* means "to go against." The word *withstand* is the same word used for antihistamine. The Lord is saying: "Stand under My rule and authority. Be in authority and under authority. Stand against the governments of hell that would resist My purposes in the earth. Let Me build your resistance to Satan's schemes in the earth.

In seasons of lost authority, we are called to return to a state of control.

Overthrow His purposes. Let Me draw near to you, and let My presence overtake you."

What should we do? First of all, find your place to stand. There are many gaps and broken places that have formed in each realm of our society. Intercessors stand. Prophets decree. Apostles execute. Get divinely aligned and stand in your assigned gap and watch as the wall of defense is rebuilt and the boundaries are extended. God's purpose was that His glory would fill the earth. Keep standing until the glory has covered your sphere of authority.

A DIVINE RECOVERY

We are living in a season and time to reclaim and recover what has been lost. To *recover* means "to recuperate or regain what has been lost or taken or to regain your health and get well." In seasons of lost authority, we are called to return to a state of control or authority.

Here are seven key issues for you to decree as you take your assigned stand. You may have lost in one season, but now decree this is the time:

1. To save yourself from falling, slipping, or being betrayed

2. To regain or reclaim land, substances from waste

3. To retrieve a person from a bad state

4. To get back by judgment

5. To return to a balance from weakness

6. To cover again

7. To reclaim or demand or decree that restoration of a thing will begin

How Do We Shift?

As we decree recovery, we are shifting our minds to think differently. The mind must think differently if we are going to enter the time we are living in and walk in victory and confidence. A transformed mind does not think like the world's blueprint (Rom. 12:1–2). Let your mind redevelop a mind-set of covenant. Worship in new ways. Do not grow comfortable, but war to enter into the rest God has for you. Let a harvest mentality of increase develop in your mind. Leave the trauma of the past behind, and begin a new, fresh season of your life. Watch your emotions! Do not let past hurts and betrayals rule you. Receive revelation about your strongholds. Know what has held you captive in the past season. Let faith arise and increase, and express your faith with actions that will topple the thrones of iniquity! Receive the angelic hosts that will lead you into a new dimension of breakthrough! Catch the *new wave* of the Holy Spirit, and come alive and *awaken* to His best!

Fourteen Issues to Embrace in the Days Ahead!

1. *This will be a season of violence.* You must understand the power of violence and become violent in the Spirit. God inhabits our praise. His habitation will make you a force in the earth. You will gain momentum and be a force to contend with in the decades to come.

2. *This will be a season of intense learning.* This will be a season of falling and getting back up. This will be a season to overcome fear. Learn to experiment for the creativity of

God to be loosed in you. God has grace for your mistakes when you are seeking to manifest His will in the earth.

3. *This will be a season to learn a different way of prospering financially.* There is a great war over wealth. Learn how to resist mammon, greed, and covetousness, and become a steward of time and money so the kingdom of God advances.

4. *This will be a season of watching.* Allow the Lord to discipline you and make you a watchman. Know who you are watching after and are connected with, and know who is watching after you. Get your assignment quickly.

5. *This will be a season in which we must understand signs.* Signs are pointers that identify and uncover godliness and the redemptive plan of God that is in the world. Do not miss your signs at this time! Do not be afraid of the supernatural, but rather begin to enter into that dimension that will get you to your new "there." This will begin individually and work into a corporate demonstration.

6. *This will be a season when we will begin to interpret supernatural revelation.* Ask God for the gift of interpretation. The Lord will be releasing a new revelation in the earth realm so you can understand times and seasons. Dreams will become very significant. There will be a revival of words of knowledge. Words of wisdom will begin to give clear directive strategy for the words of knowledge being received. These two gifts will balance each other in this season. For understanding, read Daniel 6–11.

7. *This will be a time of repositioning the army of the Lord.* There will be much shifting in the church and in the lands of the earth at this time. Many will become dissatisfied with traditionalism and will seek God's supernatural power. Therefore, God will shift many into new places.

8. *This will be a season of God's people being cleansed from pointing the finger.* There are many in the body of Christ who are critical, judgmental, negative, and condemning. Unless they are delivered, they will wander in this next season and will not be able to find their place. If you will pray Isaiah 58 and let God lead you into the type of fast that He has for you, you will be delivered and positioned properly for the future. Realign yourself! God is changing territorial boundaries.

9. *This will be a season in which God shows us how to end curses.* There are certain curses that the Lord is ready to bring to an end in the land. Joel 2 is very important. This is a time to transfer evil into blessing. Do not be afraid to face the curse that has hindered your progress. Decode the occult structure linked with the curse. Evaluate its destruction, and begin the rebuilding cycle for your future.

10. *This will be a season of walking or treading on the land of your promise.* There are new paths to be made at this time. As you walk and advance, that which does not seem to be in place will begin to become a path of light. You will also go to places you have not been to before. The Lord will begin to penetrate ungodly nations and bring His glory to places that have never experienced Him. This will be a season of pioneering into new places after judgment and wrath have occurred. This is the time when we begin to face the antichrist system that will be a hindrance to God's kingdom advancing in the earth realm. Fear not, and tread forth!

11. *This will be season of threshing.* Thresh is used figuratively in the Bible to relate to providential chastisement, crushing oppression, judicial visitation, and the labors of ministers. Grain, wine, and oil were all related to threshing, and were products of the soil. Key threshing floors in our areas must

be uncovered at this time. There is a new sound that is coming to the earth linked with threshing.

12. *This will be a season of a different type of worship than you've ever known.* Worship patterns are changing in the earth. One generation worshiped in one way, and now a new generation will lead us in worshiping in new ways. The tabernacle of David is being established. Individual worship will turn into corporate worship. Corporate worship is a key to the transformation of our regions.

13. *This will be a season where the roar of the Lion becomes very distinguishable.* The enemy will roar loudly, but the Lion of Judah will roar louder. You must learn the Lion of Judah's sound. It is in you, and it must be drawn out of you. Ferret out criminals. Psalm 101 is a key chapter. Pray this for your region, and pray that every evil thing will be exposed.

14. *This will be a season of dominion.* You will understand your sphere of authority and your assignments from God; and you will occupy, cultivate, watch after, and steward all the resources that He has given. This is a time to recognize you have a portion in the earth and to stand and decree that this land is yours!

BE SIMPLE, AND LET THIS BE YOUR TIME OF THE NEW BEGINNING

For years I have taken the Hebrew calendar and looked at the meaning of the numbers and prayed for my year to reflect His year. When we are serving the Lord and seeking His kingdom plan, I believe each year brings new challenges and new joys for each of us. The Hebrew number system has always helped me as I focus on decreeing the *best* the Lord has each year for me and my family and those connected with me. I do not think you have to understand the Hebrew year to know the will of

God. However, in Hebrew, numbers have word meanings, which have picture meanings, which have sounds. This brings a fuller perspective than just saying we have entered the year 2008. The Hebraic year 5768, which will encompass the Gregorian calendar's A.D. 2008, is *The Year of Samekh Chet!* That means we have entered *The Year of the Full Circle of Life—a New Beginning Is Yours!*

Time is an interesting concept. God is not in time as we are in time. Our Father has access to every moment in our lives from beginning to end as though they were the present. By the Holy Spirit, we can actually access those times in our pasts when we felt abandoned, abused, betrayed, fearful, happy, fulfilled, or any other emotion or condition. Not only can a believer be forgiven for the past, he or she can also face the past. The Lord can bring your past into your present so you see Him as a very present help in the midst of your past (Ps. 46:1).

> *Not only can a believer be forgiven for the past, he or she can also face the past.*

You can then redeem those past times that the enemy wanted to use for evil. You must, however, learn to respond to Him within time. You are called to represent Him as an ambassador in your generation. The decisions and actions you take now affect three generations ahead. Therefore, when you know how the Lord wants you to respond, and you do so, His glory infiltrates the earth, and you see Him change your atmosphere and environment. Because of God's position relative to time, He can—and often does—seem to answer your prayers before they have been uttered!

God has chosen you as a necessary link to bring His will from heaven to Earth. He wants you to commune with Him, listen carefully to His voice, gain prophetic revelation, and decree that revelation on the earth. This will unlock miracles and release His blessings. Once you hear God, you can intercede. You can also prophesy. Prophecy is declaring His mind and His heart. When you receive prophetic revelation, you need to decree the prophetic revelation. Then the atmosphere into which you decree goes on *heaven's time* instead of *Earth time*.

A Season of War

Issachar was the tribe that knew how to move into the new. They were a tribe that understood times and seasons. Consequently, I have tried to present that tribe in the earth today so God's children would know the times we are living in and what we should do to ready ourselves to advance in the earth. We entered a new season of war in the Hebraic year 5762. If we review the last several years, we will better understand the transitions that have been going on in our lives. By taking the time to remember, we have a good record of how we have gotten to where we are today. By looking at the Hebraic numbers, we can perceive the revelation that we need to decree a new thing. Once we decree a thing, we can then watch to see God's will manifest. Revelation builds. Revelation overcomes the gates of hell. Revelation gives us the keys to the kingdom!

Because I could foresee the war season ahead of its onset, Rebecca Wagner Sytsema and I wrote *The Future War of the Church* to help God's people get prepared with the mind-set of the season.[11] This season is very real to most of us now. Here is a summary from a Hebraic perspective of the season in which we have been living:

A Hebraic Perspective of Our Times

5762/2001–2002: The Beginning of Wars for Seven Years
This was ushered in with the tragedy of September 11, 2001, when the World Trade Center was destroyed by terrorist activities. *This war over God's covenant plan in the earth began.* The war over passing the mantle to the next generation also began.
5763/2002–2003: A Sabbath Day Rest Year
A time of increasing faith; a *year to ride the bull.* Changing economic structures began and will fully manifest over the next five years.
5764/2003–2004: The Year of *Samekh Hei*

A year filled with secrets, mysteries, and surprises; *a year to run with the horses*, gain new strength, and roar louder than the roaring lion.

5765/2004–2005: A Year to Circle, Surround, and Plunder the Enemy's Camp

A year of violent praise; a year of hurricanes; a time the wind of heaven brought change in the earth.

5766/2005–2006: The Year of *Samekh Vav*

A year of staking your claim in the midst of the whirlwind. A time to overthrow old mind-sets that have held you captive.

5767/2006–2007: The Year of *Samekh Zayin*

The year of seven is always a year of completion and fulfillment. This was a time to finish strong. The number seven, *zayin*, is a sword with a crown. How you overcame in the past season causes you to receive favor for your future. The sword is the Word, so this is a year of the prophetic decrees.

The Hebrew people equated the passage of time with the *life cycle*. They saw man as participating in two time dimensions. One *age* of time was temporal. We were placed in nature, and we interact with the laws of science around us. The other dimension of time was an age to come. First Corinthians 2:6–8 says, "However, we speak wisdom among those who are mature, yet not the wisdom of this age, nor of the rulers of this age, who are coming to nothing. But we speak the wisdom of God in a mystery, the hidden wisdom which God ordained before the ages for our glory, which none of the rulers of this age knew; for had they known, they would not have crucified the Lord of glory." Wisdom is available that God has stored for a time such as this. We can gain wisdom to which no enemy of hell has access. From a Hebraic mind-set, events that occurred through life created smaller cycles of review for a bigger picture of life. When one summed up all of these smaller temporal cycles, the finite age was determined. We are living in a season of "summing up." We are not just living from year to year, but when we look at the seven-year season as a whole, we will see the Lord doing something in our generation. He is preparing us to move more quickly and advance in kingdom purpose in days ahead.

WE ARE NOW MOVING FROM GLORY TO GLORY

You are being positioned to make a transition into the next realm of glory. Time and space around you are changing. You will begin something new. Even if you refused to shift into a visible new dimension, your present state is your new state. He will meet you where you are and cause you to start new if you yield. If you feel you are behind, you can catch up quickly and gain momentum even if you have resisted change. If you do not yield, your *new* place will be your old cycle with the old structures reinforced seven times. All transitions lead to new beginnings. The Hebrew word *chet* (from the Hebraic year 5768, the year of *Samekh Chet*) is aligned with new and linked with *life* and *being hot*! Activate your will, and choose to *be hot* and filled with passion so you conceive your future! Choose the fire and zeal of God!

Here are some decrees for you to make:

1. *Decree a manifestation.* There will be a physical manifestation of what you have been watching and waiting to see.

2. *Decree old structures, boundaries, and walls will give way to the new.* You can supernaturally transcend your limitations and begin your new era.

3. *Declare that the heavens will manifest the glory of God.* The land you are standing on and the heavens will align to create a new divine presence in your atmosphere.

4. *Decree that sin shall not have dominion over you. Dominion* will be a key word for this year. Rule where you have been positioned. Rule or you will see the "wild beasts" gain ground in your land.

5. *Decree that your mind will be energized and you will overcome.* This is a time when God's people will have great authority over their enemies. The nations against you can be driven out of your land. All squatters must go from your inheritance, or they gain "squatters' rights" and their encroachment will remain another season. Land is equated to the state of our mind. Therefore, this is the time to transform our minds so we have a new victory mentality in the war season we are living in.

6. *Subdue your animal impulses.* Find your place of deliverance and do not let any wild beast enter your highway. Be aggressive to overthrow all poverty mentality. Do not let "There is a lion on the road" be a theme that causes you to hide yourself. Stand firm and face any transgression so you can move down your path. Isaiah 35 is a key for us this year.

7. *Declare that you will renew your covenant with the Lord and advance little by little into your promise.* Do not despise small beginnings. Exodus 23 is also key for this time. God forms His covenant with us so we advance into our future destiny. This applies to families, regions, and nations. If we have forgotten and rejected His covenant in areas, that will not be a part of our future. We must return and review our covenant roots and realign now.

8. *Declare the Spirit of the Lord and you will be ONE!* Fasten yourself to the Lord. Do not let the enemy's hook drag you off the stage of your future. Break your orphan spirit. Return to a place of innocence. The secret place calls you forth. Stay in the secret place so you can be sent forth on key missions. The Book of John and all of his epistles are keys for our transitions this season.

Simplify for the Days Ahead

We are living in complicated times. Recently, my wife, Pam, shared a dream with me. You should first know that Pam's favorite Scripture passage is Ephesians 5:8–14:

> For you were once darkness, but now you are light in the Lord. Walk as children of light (for the fruit of the Spirit is in all goodness, righteousness, and truth), finding out what is acceptable to the Lord. And have no fellowship with the unfruitful works of darkness, but rather expose them. For it is shameful even to speak of those things which are done by them in secret. But all things that are exposed are made manifest by the light, for whatever makes manifest is light. Therefore He says:
> "Awake, you who sleep,
> Arise from the dead,
> And Christ will give you light."

To *redeem* means "to buy back or to be released from prison." We have been in a buying-back season. This is a time when we must receive the prize of our battles!

This is the dream she shared:

> I woke up slowly this morning to the sound of singing birds, and it was as though I was walking through a curtain that divided the dream world from the waking world. As I lay there, I began remembering my dream: I was with a group of travelers, none of whom I recognized, but I knew they were important to me. We were told we had to take a trip, but we had no luggage, tickets, or itinerary. We were standing in a hallway similar to one you might see in an airport, waiting for our departure. Suddenly, this strong wind began to blow down the hallway (wind tunnel) and push us toward the open end of the corridor. As we got closer to the end of the corridor, some kind of portal opened up, but it wasn't like what you see in the science-fiction show *Stargate*! The light was warm, and as we entered the portal area, we were disembodied and transported

to another place. Strangely, the other place didn't look any different than the place we had just been. However, it was not the same place. We were inside a building, made mostly of glass (like the Pennzoil Place in Houston, Texas).

We all knew we had to fly to get where we needed to go. Well, none of us knew how to fly, but we just took off and started flying around the lobby. The people in the lobby were amazed and started reaching for us, saying they wanted to fly too. We knew we needed more momentum to get where we needed to be, so we landed softly, turned around, and got a running start before launching ourselves from a minitrampoline in the cafe area of the lobby. Instantly we were outside the building, in a country setting, and we knew our mission: *rescue a captive in the nearby village and bring him or her back with us.*

The mission itself is still vague, but I remember what happened when we were ready to return. One of the villagers wanted to go with us but knew it wasn't possible, so he gave each of us a tiny jewel case. Mine was a small, gold case encrusted with pearls. Inside the case were bits and pieces of broken jewelry: pearls, gold beads, crystals. Each case had a word on it. The word on the outside of mine was *Simplify*. We thanked the one who gave us the gifts, then turned to launch back into the sky for the return trip. That's when the birds woke me up.

The violent are taking the kingdom of heaven by force. Certain changes in the earth have occurred in the last season that have created motion that cannot be stopped. The kingdom of darkness must give way to the kingdom of God, which is advancing with new strength. The supernatural power of God being released on His people is creating much motion and change in the earth.

We are under the impulsion or driving force of a King who wants to see change in the world today. We must gain momentum now! As we learn to move in our proper spheres of authority in the earth realm, we will harness God's power and then release that power. The season ahead will be a transforming time for God's people. Once we are transformed, we will see cities, regions, and nations changed. Harvest fields that are ripe will be entered with great enthusiasm. Do not let carnal impulses guide you.

God will visit you in time. Be expectant to watch for His coming visitation in your life. We are a people on the move. God has a kingdom that is within us. The kingdom of God is advancing. We are moving from fellowship into war. We are moving from praise to jubilation as we see a manifestation of His promises in our life cycle. This is a time of transcending and taking back what has been held in captivity. However, remember Pam's word, *Simplify*, to go back and forth with ease until the new is established. To summarize, this is a time to "go through the eye of needle." Remove all and get through your narrow place and into the new!

May you recognize that we have a God who loves to enter time today and change the space that each of us has been given to steward, cultivate, and watch after. May you be like the tribe of Issachar and understand the times and seasons, and most importantly, gain revelation to know what you should do.

NOTES

CHAPTER 1
DEVELOPING AN UNDERSTANDING OF TIME

1. Haystack Observatory, Massachusetts Institute of Technology, "The Passage of Time," http://www.haystack.mit.edu/edu/pcr/GPS/documents/the%20passage%20of%20time.htm (accessed May 21, 2007).

2. C. S. Lewis, *Mere Christianity* (San Francisco, CA: Harper-Collins Edition, 2001), 166, 170.

3. Chuck Pierce and Pamela J. Pierce, *One Thing: How to Keep Your Faith in a World of Chaos* (Shippensburg, PA: Destiny Image, 2006).

4. Dutch Sheets, public speaking.

5. Ibid.

6. Dutch Sheets and Chuck D. Pierce, *Releasing the Prophetic Destiny of a Nation* (Shippensburg, PA: Destiny Image Publishers, Inc., 2005), 91–92.

7. ScienceDaily.com, "What Is Time?" April 15, 2005, http://www.sciencedaily.com/releases/2005/04/050415115227.htm (accessed May 21, 2007).

CHAPTER 2
FEAR NOT! DEVELOPING FAITH FOR YOUR FUTURE

1. Chuck Pierce, *Reordering Your Day: Understanding and Embracing the Four Prayer Watches* (Denton, TX: Glory of Zion International Ministries, 2006).

2. Chuck Pierce and John Dickson, *The Worship Warrior: Ascending in Worship, Descending in War* (Ventura, CA: Regal Books, 2002), 209–210.

3. Arthur Burk, *Relentless Generational Blessings* (Anaheim, CA: Plumbline Ministries, 2003).

4. Dutch Sheets, *God's Timing for Your Life* (Ventura, CA: Regal Books, 2001), 16–17.

5. Chuck D. Pierce and Robert Heidler, *Restoring Your Shield of Faith* (Ventura, CA: Regal Books, 2004), 28.

6. R. T. Kendall, *Believing God* (Charlotte, NC: MorningStar Publications, 1997), 13.

7. Eliyahu Kitov, *The Book of Our Heritage, Volume Two: Adar-Nisan* (Spring Valley, NY: Feldheim Publishers, 1996), 358.

8. BlueLetterBible.org, "Dictionary and Word Search for *tiqvah* (Strong's 08615)," Blue Letter Bible, 1996–2007, http://cf .blueletterbible.org/lang/lexicon/lexicon.cfm?Strongs=H08615&Ver sion=KJV (accessed August 10, 2007).

9. Barbara J. Yoder, *The Breaker Anointing* (Ventura, CA: Regal Books, 2004), 11, 19, 21.

10. *Vine's Expository Dictionary of Old Testament Words*, PC Study Bible Version 5, copyright © 1998–2007, BIBLESOFT, Inc.

11. Chuck D. Pierce and Rebecca Wagner Sytsema, *The Future War of the Church* (Ventura, CA: Renew Books, 2001), 39–40.

12. Alfred Edersheim, *The Life and Times of Jesus the Messiah* (Grand Rapids, MI: Wm. B. Eerdmans Publishing Co., 1971), 253.

13. Ibid.

14. Ibid.

15. *American Dictionary of the English Language* (San Francisco, CA: Foundation for American Christian Education, 1987); republished facsimile edition of Noah Webster's *First Edition of an American Dictionary of the English Language*.

CHAPTER 3
IN THE PROCESS OF TIME, GOD WILL VISIT!
(DON'T GET LOST IN THE PROCESS)

1. Noah Webster, *First Edition of an American Dictionary of the English Language*. Republished in facsimile edition by the Foundation for American Christian Education, San Francisco, CA, 1987.

2. *Vine's Expository Dictionary of Old Testament Words*, PC Study Bible Version 5, copyright © 1998–2007, BIBLESOFT, Inc., s.v. "departure."

3. Kevin Wheeler, "The Power of Process," ERE.net, August 12, 2004, available at http://www.ere.net/articles/default .asp?CID={4D0A8660-FF1B-4467-AB56-50FFA76FCFD0} (accessed May 30, 2007).

4. Sheets, *God's Timing for Your Life*, 33.

5. Chuck D. Pierce and Rebecca Wagner Sytsema, *God's Now Time for Your Life* (Ventura, CA: Regal Books, 2005), 27–28.

CHAPTER 4
THERE WILL COME A DAY

1. Spiros Zodhiates, *The Hebrew-Greek Key Word Study Bible, New American Standard Bible* (Chattanooga, TN: AMG Publishers, 1977), 1710.

2. Sheets and Pierce, *Releasing the Prophetic Destiny of a Nation*, 109–110.

3. Zodhiates, *The Hebrew-Greek Key Word Study Bible, New American Standard Bible*, 1712.

4. Sheets and Pierce, *Releasing the Prophetic Destiny of a Nation*, 111.

5. Ibid., 82.

6. "O Come, O Come, Emmanuel," translated from Latin to English by John M. Neale. Public domain. Lyrics from Cyberhymnal.org, "O Come, O Come, Emmanuel," http://www.cyberhymnal.org/htm/o/c/ocomocom.htm (accessed August 14, 2007).

7. Chuck D. Pierce and Rebecca Wagner Sytsema, *When God Speaks* (Ventura, CA: Regal Books, 2005), 108.

8. Wesley Campbell, *Welcoming a Visitation of the Holy Spirit* (Lake Mary, FL: Charisma House, 1996), 60.

9. Pierce and Sytsema, *When God Speaks*, 43–73.

CHAPTER 5
FROM ONE NARROW TRANSITION TO ANOTHER:
A KINGDOM ON THE MOVE

1. Lyrics by Chuck Pierce, John Dickson, music by John Dickson, "I See a Light," *Go Up Again!* CD (Glory of Zion International Ministries, Inc, 2007), printed with permission.

2. Pierce and Pierce, *One Thing*.

3. Ibid., 39–41.

4. Personal communication.

5. Pierce and Dickson, *The Worship Warrior*, 158–160.

6. Ibid., 176.

7. Bob Sorge, *Exploring Worship: A Practical Guide to Praise and Worship* (Greenwood, MO: Oasis House, 1987, 2001), 7.

8. Don McMinn, *Entering His Presence: Experiencing the Joy of True Worship* (South Plainfield, NJ: Bridge Publishing, Inc., 1986), 53.

9. Darlene Zschech, *Extravagant Worship* (Castle Hill, NSW, Australia, 2001), 64.

10. Robert Gay, *Silencing the Enemy* (Lake Mary, FL: Charisma House, 1993), 16.

11. Wikipedia.org, *Coup de grâce*, http://en.wikipedia.org/wiki/Coup_de_grace (accessed June 16, 2007).

12. From WordNet © 2.1, Princeton University, 01 Mar. 2007, dictionary.com.

13. Matt Redman, *The Unquenchable Worshipper: Coming Back to the Heart of Worship* (Ventura, CA: Regal Books, 2001), 44.

14. Ivan Engnell, *Studies in Divine Kingship in the Ancient Near East* (1943); Henri Frankfort, *Kingship and the Gods* (1948); A. R. Johnson, *Sacral Kingship in Ancient Israel* (1955); G. E. Mendenhall, *Law and Covenant in Israel and the Ancient Near East* (1955); K. W. Whitelaw (from *The New Unger's Bible Dictionary*. Originally published by Moody Press of Chicago, Illinois (Copyright © 1988).

15. Lewis Sperry Chafer, *Systematic Theology*, 7:224; cited in *New Unger's Bible Dictionary*, originally published by Moody Press of Chicago, IL, 1988 found on PC Study Bible version 5.

CHAPTER 6
A TIME TO BE POSITIONED FOR YOUR FUTURE

1. Chuck Missler, "The Wilderness Wanderings," *Koinonia House Online*, at http://www.khouse.org/articles/2006/631/ (accessed June 26, 2007).

2. Albert Einstein in a letter to his son, Eduard Einstein, February 5, 1930. Courtesy of Barbara Wolff, Einstein archives, Hebrew University, Jerusalem. Quoted from Walter Isaacson, *Einstein: His Life and Universe* (New York: Simon & Schuster, 2007), ix.

3. From Lesson 1: "The Impulse-Momentum Change Theorem," *The Physics Classroom*, at http://www.glenbrook.k12.il.us/gbssci/phys/Class/momentum/u4l1b.html, accessed June 27, 2007.

4. Pierce and Sytsema, *God's Now Time for Your Life*.

5. First Fruits of Zion, "Trumpets and Clouds," *The Weekly eDrash*, http://ffoz.org/resources/edrash/behaalotcha/?zoom_highlight=trumpets+and+clouds (accessed December 5, 2007).

CHAPTER 7
THROUGH TO THE NEW: TRAVAIL, ORDER AND TIME

1. Sheets and Pierce, *Releasing the Prophetic Destiny of a Nation*, 101–102.

2. Monte Judah, "The Oil of Anointing," *Yavoh, He is Coming* newsletter, April 2006, Lion and Lamb Ministries, PO Box 720968, Norman, OK 73070.

3. Ibid.

4. Ibid.

5. Pierce and Pierce, *One Thing*.

6. Adapted from "Word of the Month," *Biblical Hebrew E-magazine*, http://www.ancient-hebrew.org/emagazine/004.doc (accessed July 11, 2007).

7. Pierce, *Reordering Your Day*.

8. William Strauss and Neil Howe, *The Fourth Turning* (New York: Broadway, 1997).

9. Ibid., 25–38.

10. Personal communication.

11. Charles G. Finney, *Lectures on Revival* (Minneapolis, MN: Bethany, 1988), 46.

12. Cindy Jacobs, *Possessing the Gates of the Enemy*, (Tarrytown, NY: Chosen Books, 1991), 115–116.

13. Personal communication.

14. Jacobs, *Possessing the Gates of the Enemy*, 116.

15. Adapted from Chuck D. Pierce and Rebecca Wagner Sytsema, *Prayers That Outwit the Enemy!* (Ventura, CA: Regal Books, 2004), 81–93.

CHAPTER 8
MAKING IT THROUGH NARROW TRANSITIONS

1. Sandie Freed, "Times of Transition—Breakthroughs in New Ways," *The Elijah List*, posted September 19, 2006, at http://www.elijahlist.com/words/display_word/4499 (accessed July 17, 2007).

2. Al Hollingsworth, *Vertical Leap* (Chino, CA: Boss Global, 2002).

3. Ibid., 31–32.

4. Ibid., 34.

5. Robert M. Haralick, *The Inner Meaning of the Hebrew Letters* (Northdale, NJ: Jason Aronson, Inc.), 129–130.

6. Ibid., 72–73.

7. Herbert Lockyer, editor, *Nelson's Illustrated Bible Dictionary* (Nashville, TN: Thomas Nelson Publishers, 1986).

8. *International Standard Bible Encyclopaedia*, Electronic Database, Copyright 1996, 2003 by Biblesoft, Inc.

9. *Fausset's Bible Dictionary*, Electronic Database, Copyright 1998 by Biblesoft, Inc.

10. Tim Hegg, "HaShem—Bringing Us Into His Abode," http://www.torahresource.com/Parashpdfs/97CommentsTR.pdf (accessed May 21, 2007). Used by permission.

11. Pierce and Sytsema, *The Future War of the Church*.